Englisn Year 9

Susan Elkin

Editor: Anthony Haynes

GALORE PARK

www.galorepark.co.uk

Published by Galore Park Publishing Ltd
19/21 Sayers Lane, Tenterden, Kent TN30 6BW
www.galorepark.co.uk

Design by River Design, Edinburgh
Typography by Typetechnique, London W1
Illustration by Rowan Barnes-Murphy

Printed by Lego S.p.A., Italy

ISBN-13: 978 1 905735 310

First published 2009

Details of other Galore Park publications are available at
www.galorepark.co.uk

ISEB Revision Guides, publications and examination papers may also be
obtained from Galore Park.

Photo credits: p2 Mary Evans Picture Library/Alamy, p7 Time Life
Pictures/Mansell/Getty Images, p21 The Print Collector/Heritage Image
Partnership, p29 Tom Duffy, p44 Keystone/Hulton Archive/Getty Images,
p49 Illustration for the extract from Coleridge's 'The Rime of the Ancient
Mariner' is by David Jones and reproduced by kind permission of The
Trustees of the Estate of David Jones, p66 akg-images, p70 Renaissance
Films/BBC/Curzon F/akg-images, p88 Krys Bailey/Alamy, p89 Tony Hamblin/
Royal Society for the Protection of Birds, p101 Musee des Beaux-Arts, Lille,
France/Lauros/Giraudon/Bridgeman Art Library, p108 The Print Collector
/Alamy, p110 Bob Thomas/Popperfoto/Getty Images, p120 Alison
Wright/National Geographic/Getty Images, p125 Dinodia Images/Alamy,
p141 Rank/Album/akg-images, p150 Kay Chernush/The Image Bank/Getty
Images, p152 Alastair Muir/Rex Features, p164 © Margaret Copley/
Bridgeman Art Library, p172 Fine Art Photographic Library/Corbis UK Ltd.,
p190 Dreamworks SKG/MacDonald/Parke/akg-images, p193 Heinrich
Hoffmann/Keystone Features/Hulton Archive/Getty Images.

Acknowledgements

**Lucas and Felix Elkin
with love**

Sincere thanks to my editor Anthony Haynes for his wise, sensitive and thorough guidance. I also thank the team at Galore Park for having faith in this project and making it happen with their usual expert efficiency. My husband, Nicholas Elkin is my first critic and proofreader and an invaluable, long-suffering sounding board for ideas. Thanks, Nick – as ever.

The publishers are grateful to the following for permission to use the extracts:

Affinity by Sarah Waters, published by Virago, used by kind permission of Little, Brown Book Group Ltd; Copyright © Sarah Waters, 1999; from *Affinity* by Sarah Waters. Copyright © 1999 by Sarah Waters. Used by permission of Riverhead Books, an imprint of Penguin Group (USA) Inc.; from *An Evil Cradling* by Brian Keenan, published by Hutchinson. Reprinted by permission of The Random House Group Ltd; permission sought for US and Canadian rights; Guardian article permission sought; 'Cleator Moor' by Norman Nicholson from *Five Rivers* and *Collected Poems*, published by Faber & Faber; 'Sonnet for South Crofty' by Elsie Balme, used by kind permission of the author; *The Kon-Tiki Expedition* permission sought; 'A Love Child' by Doris Lessing from *The Grandmothers*. Reprinted by permission of HarperCollins Publishers Ltd © Doris Lessing, 2003; permission sought for USA and Canadian rights; 'Survivors' permission sought; extract from *Viking Girl* by Pauline Chandler (OUP, 2007), copyright © Pauline Chandler 2007, reprinted by permission of Oxford University Press; *War in Korea…* permission sought; Michael McCarthy, 2008 © The Independent, 15 January 2008; *The Life of Birds* by David Attenborough, by kind permission of the author; *The Drunken Forest*, produced with permission of Curtis Brown Group Ltd, London, on behalf of the Estate of Gerald Durrell. Copyright © Gerald Durrell 1956; 'Thrushes' permission sought; 'Thrushes' from *Lupercal* from *Selected Poems 1957-1994* by Ted Hughes. Copyright © 2002 by The Estate of Ted Hughes. Reprinted by permission of Farrar, Straus and Giroux, LLC; 'Cock-Pheasant' from *Selected Poems*. Reprinted by permission of United Agents on behalf of The Estate of Laurie Lee © as printed in the original volume; from *Things Fall Apart* by Chinua Achebe. Reprinted by permission of Pearson Education; *Girl with a Pearl Earring* © 1999 Tracey Chevalier, by kind permission of HarperCollins Publishers Ltd; reproduced with permission of Curtis Brown Group Ltd London on behalf of Tracy Chevalier, copyright © Tracy Chevalier 1999; Clover Stroud, 2008 © The Daily Telegraph, 7 January 2008; *A Fine Balance* by Rohinton Mistry, published by Faber and Faber Ltd; *The Jewel in the Crown* by Paul Scott, published by Heinemann; extract from *Basil Street Blues* reproduced by kind permission of A P Watt Ltd on behalf of Michael Holroyd; Josef Stawinoga © The Telegraph, 17 November 2007; 'Old People's Nursing Home' by Elizabeth Jennings from *New Collected Poems*, published by Carcanet; Gerald Berkowitz, 2007, by kind permission © The Stage, 29th November 2007; excerpt from 'Alexander Fleming' by Michael Warboys, from the *Oxford Dictionary of National Biography* (2004). By permission of Oxford University Press; Eve Curie © The Telegraph, 8 November 2007; extract from 'Doing Science in the Bath' from *1000 Inventions and Discoveries* edited by Roger Bridgman and published by Dorling Kindersley in 2006. Copyright © Dorling Kindersely, 2006. Reproduced by permission of Penguin Books Ltd; extract from *The Time Machine* reproduced by kind permission of A P Watt Ltd on behalf of The Literary Executors of the Estate of HG Wells; 'Dissection' permission sought; Gail Campbell Thomson, 2008 © Liverpool Daily Post, 25th January 2008; excerpts from *King Leopold's Ghost* by Adam Hochschild. Copyright © 1998 by Adam Hochschild. Reprinted by permission of Houghton Mifflin Harcourt Publishing Company. All rights reserved.

Contents

English Year 9

Introduction xii

Chapter 1 Behind Bars 1
Writing about literature 12
Personal writing 12
Word bank 13
Nuts and bolts 14
Get it right 16
More speaking and listening activities 17
Just for fun 17
Wide range reading 18
Moving on 19
Ready for a real challenge? 19

Chapter 2 Mining, Mines and Miners 20
Writing about literature 31
Personal writing 32
Word bank 33
Nuts and bolts (1) 34
Nuts and bolts (2) 36
Get it right 36
More speaking and listening activities 38
Just for fun 39
Wide range reading 39
Moving on 40
Ready for a real challenge? 40

Chapter 3 All at Sea 41
Writing about literature 53
Personal writing 54
Word bank 54
Nuts and bolts 56
Get it right 58

Contents

More speaking and listening activities 59

Just for fun 59

Wide range reading 60

Moving on 61

Ready for a real challenge? 61

Chapter 4 Let Slip the Dogs of War 62

Writing about literature 72

Personal writing 73

Word bank 74

Nuts and bolts 75

Get it right 76

More speaking and listening activities 78

Just for fun 79

Wide range reading 79

Moving on 81

Ready for a real challenge? 81

Chapter 5 All the Birds of the Air 82

Writing about literature 91

Personal writing 92

Word bank 92

Nuts and bolts 94

Get it right 95

More speaking and listening activities 97

Just for fun 98

Wide range reading 98

Moving on 99

Ready for a real challenge? 99

Chapter 6 The World of Work 100

Writing about literature 111

Personal writing 111

Contents

Word bank 112

Nuts and bolts 113

Get it right 114

More speaking and listening activities 116

Just for fun 116

Wide range reading 117

Moving on 118

Ready for a real challenge? 118

Chapter 7 A Passage to India 119

Writing about literature 128

Personal writing 129

Word bank 129

Nuts and bolts (1) 131

Nuts and bolts (2) 133

Get it right 135

More speaking and listening activities 136

Just for fun 137

Wide range reading 137

Moving on 139

Ready for a real challenge? 139

Chapter 8 Age Cannot Wither Her 140

Writing about literature 153

Personal writing 153

Word bank 154

Nuts and bolts 155

Get it right 158

More speaking and listening activities 159

Just for fun 160

Wide range reading 160

Moving on 161

Ready for a real challenge? 161

Contents

Chapter 9 Eureka! 162

Writing about literature 178

Personal writing 178

Word bank 179

Nuts and bolts 181

Get it right 183

More speaking and listening activities 184

Just for fun 185

Wide range reading 185

Moving on 187

Ready for a real challenge? 187

Chapter 10 Subtle, False and Treacherous 188

Writing about literature 203

Personal writing 204

Word bank 205

Nuts and bolts 206

Get it right 207

More speaking and listening activities 209

Just for fun 210

Wide range reading 210

Moving on 212

Ready for a real challenge? 212

Appendix: Puzzle solutions 213

English is an extraordinary subject. Unlike science, geography or history it has no body of knowledge to study or theories to test. Unlike maths it offers few definite answers. Unlike music it isn't aural. Unlike art it isn't visual. Unlike PE it doesn't make you sweat.

Instead, English, which is so much more than a language, is about words, ideas, communication and, of course, books: novels, short stories, non-fiction, poetry, plays and anything else you can put in a book. Reading is the backbone of English and, of course, not all reading comes from books. Newspapers, magazines, information leaflets, instructions, reports, internet sites, emails and text messages all have to be read too.

English is both an umbrella and a sponge. It arches over all other subjects. Whatever you are doing in school at any time of the day you will be reading, writing, speaking and/or listening – using what you learn in English lessons.

On the other hand, it soaks up subject matter from every other area of the curriculum. When you read the extract from Sarah Waters's *Affinity* in Chapter 1 of this book you are also studying history. The passage from David Attenborough's *Life of Birds* in Chapter 5 takes you into science and most of the extracts about ageing in Chapter 8 into sociology, PSHE and citizenship. There are examples of these links between subjects on almost every page.

To get the best out of this glitteringly exciting subject and wonderfully diverse, slippery language of ours you need the best possible knowledge of it so that you use it as skilfully and confidently as you can. That is why each chapter has sections on English's 'nuts and bolts' and exercises to encourage you to learn new words and spell them correctly. I've also given you dozens of writing suggestions and ideas for practising those vital speaking and listening skills.

But it's books which dominate *English Year 9*. A 2003 survey across Europe confirmed what teachers already knew and have been telling pupils since schools were invented: that, although a number of things affect how well you do at school, it is the reading of books which makes the biggest difference. In other words, the more books you read the more progress you are likely to make in all your subjects.

So try some of the books from which the extracts come. They are a very varied selection but every one of them is a fine book in its own way. Read some of the dozens of titles listed towards the end of each chapter too. It shouldn't be a hardship. There are some really great reads on these lists. And the joy of reading is that it's a treasure hunt-like adventure because every book you finish leads you on to another one.

If you get half the fun from reading and using this book that I have had in putting it together you, like me, are very lucky.

Up with English!

Susan Elkin, March 2009

Have you ever passed a prison? What did you notice about it? How did being near it make you feel? You have probably also seen films and dramas or documentaries on television which feature prisons so most of us have some idea what a prison is like.

In this chapter we explore some fine literature and language by thinking about imprisonment, not in Britain in the 21st century, but elsewhere and at other times under other circumstances. In Passage B, for instance, the imprisoned man has not been jailed by the state. He is a hostage held by terrorists.

Read the two passages below. Then do the written tasks which follow.

Passage A

In this fascinating and very readable modern novel the narrator visits the women's section of a nineteenth century prison at Millbank in London. Sarah Waters is very good at making all the details of Victorian Britain come alive – however chilling. She also has an exciting knack of springing totally unexpected surprises in her story telling.

It was an impressive thing to see. As I had arrived there had been a tolling of the prison bell: when the matrons of the wards hear that they must each take four women from their cells and walk with them to the prison kitchen. We found them gathered at its door when we went up to them: Miss Manning, Mrs Pretty, Mrs Jelf and twelve pale prisoners, the prisoners with their eyes upon the floor and their hands before them. The women's building has no kitchen of its own, but takes its dinners from the men's gaol. Since the male and female wards are kept quite separate, the women are obliged to wait very quietly until the men have taken their soup and the kitchen is cleared. Miss Ridley explained this to me. 'They must not see the men', she said. 'Those are the rules.' As she spoke there came, from behind the bolted kitchen door, the slither of heavy-booted feet, the murmurs – and I had a sudden vision then of the men as *goblin* men, with snouts and tails and whiskers …

Then the sounds grew less, and Miss Ridley lifted her keys to give a knock upon the wood: 'All clear, Mr Lawrence?' The answer came – 'All clear!' – and the door was unfastened, to let the prisoners file through. The warder-cook stood by with his arms folded, watching the women and sucking at his cheek.

The kitchen seemed vast to me, and terribly warm after the chill, dark passage. Its air was thick, the scents on it not wonderful; they have sand upon the floor, and this was dark and clogged with fallen fluid. Down the centre of the room were ranged three broad tables, and on those were placed the women's cans of soup and meat and trays of loaves. Miss Ridley waved the prisoners forward, two by two, and each

seized the can or the tray for her ward, and
staggered away with it. I walked back with Miss
Manning's women. We found the prisoners of the
ground-floor cells all ready at their gates, holding
35 their tin mugs and their trenchers, and while
soup was ladled out the matron called a prayer –
'God-bless-our-meat-and-make-us-worthy-of-it!'
or some rough thing like that – the women
seemed almost to ignore her. They only stood
40 very quietly and pressed their faces to their gates,
in an attempt to catch the progress of their
dinners down the ward. When the dinners came
they turned and carried them to their tables, then
daintily sprinkled salt upon them from the boxes
45 on their shelves.

*A prisoner at work in her cell in
Fulham female prison, 1875*

They were given a meat soup with potatoes, and
a six-ounce loaf – all of it horrible: the loaves
coarse and brown and over-baked as little bricks, the potatoes boiled in their skins
and streaked with black. The soup was cloudy, and had a layer of grease upon the
50 top that thickened and whitened as the cans grew cool. The meat was pale, and too
gristly for the women's dull-edged knives to leave much mark upon it: I saw many
prisoners tearing at their mutton with their teeth, solemn as savages.

They stood and took it readily enough, however; some only seemed to gaze rather
mournfully at the soup as it was ladled out, others to finger their meat with
55 suspicion. 'Don't you care for your dinner?' I asked one woman handling her mutton
like this. She answered that she didn't care to think upon whose hands might have
been on it, in the men's gaol.

'They handles filthy things', she said, 'then jiggles their fingers in our soup, for sport …'

She said this two or three times, then would not talk to me. I left her mumbling into
60 her mug, and joined the matrons at the entrance to the ward.

I talked a little with Miss Ridley then, about the women's diet and the variations
that are made in it – there being always fish served on a Friday, for example, on
account of the large numbers of Roman Catholic prisoners; and on a Sunday, suet
pudding. I said, had they any Jewesses, and she answered that there were always a
65 number of Jewesses, and they liked to make 'a particular trouble' over the
preparation of their dishes. She had encountered that sort of behaviour, amongst
the Jewesses, at other prisons.

From *Affinity* by Sarah Waters (1999)

>> Task 1.1

1. Choose and comment on three words or phrases from Passage A which strike you as particularly interesting and/or well chosen.

2. Summarise the eating arrangements for the women prisoners. Use your own words but incorporate short quotations (using inverted commas) from the passage into your sentences.

3. What impression do you get of the narrator from her words and attitude? Look particularly closely at her conversation with the 'woman handling her mutton like this' and write in as much detail as you can.

1

Passage B

The narrator of this autobiographical account was kidnapped and held prisoner for four and a half years by militant Muslims in Beirut in the late 1980s. Perhaps because he is a university English teacher (he was teaching at the University of Beirut when he was taken) Brian Keenan uses language with extraordinary sensitivity and flair.

5

10

Another day. The Shuffling Acolyte and I take part in our daily ritual, that long short walk to the toilet. That same walk back and I am home again. I don't look any more at the food, knowing its monotony will not change, nor its place on my filthy floor. The door closes, the padlock rattling, and it's over again for another day. With calm, disinterested deliberation I pull from my

head the filthy towel that blinds me, and slowly turn to go like a dog well-trained to its
15   corner, to sit again and wait and wait, forever waiting. I look at this food I know to be the same as it always has been.

But wait. My eyes are almost burned by what I see. There's a bowl in front of me that wasn't there before. A brown button bowl and in it some apricots, some small oranges, some nuts, cherries, a banana. The fruits, the colours, mesmerize me in a
20   quiet rapture that spins through my head. I am entranced by colour. I lift an orange into the flat filthy palm of my hand and feel and smell and lick it. The colour orange, the colour, the colour, my God the colour orange. Before me is a feast of colour. I feel myself begin to dance, slowly, I am intoxicated by colour. I feel the colour in a quiet somnambulant rage. Such wonder, such absolute wonder in such an insignificant fruit.

25   I cannot. I will not eat this fruit. I sit in quiet joy, so complete, beyond the meaning of joy. My soul finds its own completeness in that bowl of colour. The forms of each

30 fruit. The shape and curl and bend all so rich, so perfect. I want to bow before it. Loving that blazing, roaring, orange colour … Everything meeting in a moment of colour and form, my rapture no longer abstract euphoria. It is there in that tiny bowl, the world recreated in that broken bowl. I feel the smell of each fruit leaping into me and lifting me and carrying me away. I am drunk with something that I understand but cannot explain. I am filled with a sense of love. I am filled and satiated by it. What I have waited and longed for has without my knowing come to me, and taken all of me.

35 For days I sit in a kind of dreamy lethargy, in part contemplation and in part worship. The walls seem to be singing. I focus all of my attention on the bowl of fruit. At times I fondle the fruits, at times I rearrange them, but I cannot eat them. I cannot hold the ecstasy of the moment and its passionate intensity. It seems to drift slowly from me as the place in which I am being held comes back to remind me of where I am and of my

40 condition. But my containment does not oppress me. I sit and look at the walls but now this room seems so expansive, it seems I can push the walls away from me. I can reach out and touch them from where I sit and yet they are so far from me.

The moment dwindles and dims like a dying fire. I begin to plot and plan and try to find a direction for my thinking. There are strange occasions when I find myself

45 thinking of two different and completely unrelated things simultaneously. I can grasp and understand the difference and the conceptual depth in each. They neither cross over nor blur into each other. They do not confuse me. I can ask and answer questions on each of these very different subjects at one and the same moment. My mind now moves into strange abstractions. The idea, the concept of time enthrals

50 me. I build a complicated and involved structure which redefines what time is. Time is different now. Its flux and pattern is new, seeming so clear, so precise, so deeply understood yet inexplicable. I am calm and quiet. The manic alternations between despair and euphoria seem to have less potency. When I feel them coming I can set aside and prevent their theft of my understanding. They can no longer master me,

55 nor drive me where they will. Now I know them and can go with them and hold them in my control.

Today I am returned to my cell and as the door closes I sit in my corner and wait for the guard to go. But today the door is opened again. I sit, my face draped in my towel. The Grim Reaper squats before me and with his faulty English asks 'Why don't

60 you eat?' I look down to see his hand hold the bowl of fruit under the towel. 'Why don't you eat?' he asks again. I feel the hopelessness of trying to explain to him. He doesn't have enough English to understand. How can I, in any case, explain what is only understood in my senses and not in my mind? I shrug. I say I do not want to eat. There is silence. Then I feel him rise and move as if to leave my cell and take the

65 bowl with him.

From *An Evil Cradling* by Brian Keenan (1992)

>> Task 1.2

1 a. What do you think Brian Keenan means by 'dreamy lethargy'?

1 b. How is he coping with the slow passing of time during his imprisonment?

2. How did the fruit affect the author and why was it so significant?

3. In this passage Brian Keenan uses the present tense to describe past events. What effect is he aiming for and how well do you think it works? Answer in as much detail as you can and quote some of the author's words (using inverted commas) in your own sentences.

>> Task 1.3

Passage A and Passage B are of different genres: the first is fiction and the second is not.

- Think carefully about the difference this makes to the way language is used and discuss it with a partner.

- Consider and discuss ways in which the two passages are similar and identify anything they have in common. Then examine ways in which they are different.

- Look at the style, words used, tone and attitude. Think about, for example, from whose point of view you are to see events in either extract.

- Make notes. It might help you to arrange your notes in two columns entitled 'Similarities' and 'Differences'.

- Then write an essay using the title 'Compare and contrast the extract from *Affinity* with the passage from *The Evil Cradling'.

Read these passages of poetry carefully. The first two are extracts from longer poems. The third is a complete poem.

Passage C

Playwright Oscar Wilde, most famous for the hilarious, highly observant play, The Importance of Being Earnest (1895) served two years in prison in the 1890s for homosexuality - a crime until the 1960s. Sentenced to 'hard labour' he died soon after his release, aged only 46. The long poem this extract comes from was inspired by his gruelling prison experience.

III

1   In Debtors' Yard the stones are hard,
And the dripping wall is high,
So it was there he took the air
Beneath the leaden sky,
5   And by each side a Warder walked,
For fear the man might die.

Or else he sat with those who watched
His anguish night and day;
Who watched him when he rose to weep,
10   And when he crouched to pray;
Who watched him lest himself should rob
Their scaffold of its prey.

The Governor was strong upon
The Regulations Act:
15   The Doctor said that Death was but
A scientific fact:
And twice a day the Chaplain called
And left a little tract.

And twice a day he smoked his pipe,
20   And drank his quart of beer:
His soul was resolute, and held
No hiding-place for fear;
He often said that he was glad
The hangman's hands were near.

25   But why he said so strange a thing
     No Warder dared to ask:
     For he to whom a watcher's doom
     Is given as his task,
     Must set a lock upon his lips,
30   And make his face a mask.

     Or else he might be moved, and try
     To comfort or console:
     And what should Human Pity do
     Pent up in Murderers' Hole?
35   What word of grace in such a place
     Could help a brother's soul?

     With slouch and swing around the ring
     We trod the Fool's Parade!
     We did not care: we knew we were
40   The Devil's Own Brigade:
     And shaven head and feet of lead
     Make a merry masquerade.

Oscar Wilde photographed in
1895, the year of his trial

     We tore the tarry rope to shreds
     With blunt and bleeding nails;
45   We rubbed the doors, and scrubbed the floors,
     And cleaned the shining rails:
     And, rank by rank, we soaped the plank,
     And clattered with the pails.

     We sewed the sacks, we broke the stones,
50   We turned the dusty drill:
     We banged the tins, and bawled the hymns,
     And sweated on the mill:
     But in the heart of every man
     Terror was lying still.

55   So still it lay that every day
     Crawled like a weed-clogged wave:
     And we forgot the bitter lot
     That waits for fool and knave,
     Till once, as we tramped in from work,
60   We passed an open grave.

With yawning mouth the yellow hole
Gaped for a living thing;
The very mud cried out for blood
To the thirsty asphalt ring:
65   And we knew that ere one dawn grew fair
Some prisoner had to swing.

Right in we went, with soul intent
On Death and Dread and Doom:
The hangman, with his little bag,
70   Went shuffling through the gloom
And each man trembled as he crept
Into his numbered tomb.

From 'The Ballad of Reading Gaol' by Oscar Wilde (1898)

Passage D

The narrator in Lord Byron's very appealing poem is a religious political prisoner in a castle dungeon in Switzerland. No one is quite sure whether this long poem is based on a real incident or whether it is fictional. The opening of this passage is often quoted.

1   My hair is grey, but not with years,
      Nor grew it white
      In a single night,
As men's have grown from sudden fears:
5   My limbs are bow'd, though not with toil,
      But rusted with a vile repose,
For they have been a dungeon's spoil,
      And mine has been the fate of those
To whom the goodly earth and air
10   Are bann'd, and barr'd—forbidden fare;
But this was for my father's faith
I suffer'd chains and courted death;
That father perish'd at the stake
For tenets he would not forsake;
15   And for the same his lineal race

In darkness found a dwelling place;
We were seven—who now are one,
    Six in youth, and one in age,
Finish'd as they had begun,
20   Proud of Persecution's rage;
One in fire, and two in field,
Their belief with blood have seal'd,
Dying as their father died,
For the God their foes denied;-
25 Three were in a dungeon cast,
Of whom this wreck is left the last.

II
There are seven pillars of Gothic mould,
In Chillon's dungeons deep and old,
There are seven columns, massy and grey,
30 Dim with a dull imprison'd ray,
A sunbeam which hath lost its way,
And through the crevice and the cleft
Of the thick wall is fallen and left;
Creeping o'er the floor so damp,
35 Like a marsh's meteor lamp:
And in each pillar there is a ring,
    And in each ring there is a chain;
That iron is a cankering thing,
    For in these limbs its teeth remain,
40 With marks that will not wear away,
Till I have done with this new day,
Which now is painful to these eyes,
Which have not seen the sun so rise
For years—I cannot count them o'er,
45 I lost their long and heavy score
When my last brother droop'd and died,
And I lay living by his side.

From 'The Prisoner of Chillon' by Lord Byron (1816)

Passage E

The poet/narrator was imprisoned for presenting a petition to King Charles I in 1642 - a time of great political unrest and civil war which led, eventually, to the execution of the king in 1649. This beautiful poem was probably written to Richard Lovelace's wife during his imprisonment. The first two lines of the fourth verse create one of the most perceptive statements ever made about imprisonment. Notice how gloriously simple these twelve words are compared with the profound idea they express.

To Althea, from Prison

1   WHEN Love with unconfined wings
     Hovers within my gates,
   And my divine Althea brings
     To whisper at the grates;
5   When I lie tangled in her hair
     And fetter'd to her eye,
   The birds that wanton in the air
     Know no such liberty.

   When flowing cups run swiftly round
10   With no allaying Thames,
   Our careless heads with roses bound,
     Our hearts with loyal flames;
   When thirsty grief in wine we steep,
     When healths and draughts go free—
15   Fishes that tipple in the deep
     Know no such liberty.

   When, like committed linnets, I
     With shriller throat shall sing
   The sweetness, mercy, majesty,
20   And glories of my King;
   When I shall voice aloud how good
     He is, how great should be,
   Enlarged winds, that curl the flood,
     Know no such liberty.

25 Stone walls do not a prison make,
        Nor iron bars a cage;
    Minds innocent and quiet take
        That for an hermitage;
    If I have freedom in my love
30   And in my soul am free,
    Angels alone, that soar above,
        Enjoy such liberty.

'To Althea, from Prison' by Richard Lovelace (1642)

>> Task 1.4

1. Summarise the prisoners' biggest shared worry in Passage C.

2a. Explain in as much detail as you can what the prisoner in Passage B means by 'vile repose'. Use short one-, two- or three-word quotations (in inverted commas) from the poem in your answer, weaving them into your sentences.

 b. How does the 'vile repose' differ from the experience of the prisoners in 'Reading Gaol' in Passage C?

3. In Passage E what is Lovelace's main view about being in prison? Contrast this with the view expressed in one of the other poetry passages: C or D, or in the prose passages: A or B.

4. Ranging across Passages C, D and E pick:

 a. five examples of alliteration (words starting with same sound)

 b. three examples of rhyme at the end of lines

 c. three examples of rhyme within lines (internal rhyme) and say how they add to the meaning and mood of the poem they come from.

5. Which of these three poems do you like most? Explain why in as much detail as you can.

6. Which poem appeals to you least? Use short quotations from the poem – in inverted commas within your sentences – to explain your reasons.

Writing about literature

Some students find it difficult to write about their reading, particularly when it is poetry. One tip is to focus on the detail. Then write about it in as much depth as you can. Study this example which comments on just four lines of 'To Althea, from Prison':

> Richard Lovelace's comparison of himself with caged birds ('committed linnets') effectively reinforces the main argument of this poem which is that imprisonment will not silence him nor take away his status as a human being. Linnet-like he will continue to 'sing' with a 'shriller throat'. He is also adamant that he will go on praising the king. The series of abstract nouns 'sweetness', 'mercies', 'majesty' and 'glories' have a determined dignity about them. In four words he conveys a very rounded picture of a king who can be gentle as well as imperious.

>> Task 1.5

Choose any four lines from any of the poems in this chapter and write a paragraph commenting on them in detail.

Personal Writing

>> Task 1.6

1. Write a story or essay inspired by Richard Lovelace's famous lines 'Stone walls do not a prison make,/ Nor iron bars a cage.'

2. Imagine you are one of the men guarding Brian Keenan in Beirut. Write a letter to a close friend about the man you are holding and your feelings about the situation.

3. Invent a story for the woman 'handling her mutton' in the prison described in *Affinity*. What is her crime? Does she have a family? What has happened to her in prison? Is she well or ill? What will happen to her later? Write in either the first person (I) or the third person (she).

4. What have you learned from these five passages about how people's minds are affected by being imprisoned? Assemble the information in a factual essay.

5. Write a newspaper article expressing your views about the use of prison as a punishment. Think about the sorts of criminal who should, or should not, be locked up, how they should be treated while they are in prison and the cost to the country of running prisons. Use any information you can find in newspapers or on the internet to help you with examples.

6. Write a poem about someone who is, for some reason, locked up and denied his or her freedom.

7. Write about imprisonment in any way you wish.

Writing tip

Plan your writing in outline before you begin to write. Think of five or six main points you want to make – or things which will happen in your story. Decide how you will begin and how you will end. Use this as a framework. Put the detail in as you write.

WORD BANK

In Passage B Brian Keenan uses the word **somnambulant**. It means **sleep walking** and comes from *somnus*, the Latin for sleep and the Latin word *ambulare* (to walk).

English also takes several words from the Latin verbs *loquor* – to speak – and *sedere* – to sit.

>> Task 1.7

Find out the meanings of these words (if you don't already know them) and use them in sentences of your own:

1. ambulant
2. sedentary
3. somnolent
4. sedate
5. loquacious
6. funambulist
7. amble
8. somniloquy
9. preamble
10. eloquent

>> Task 1.8

Use a dictionary to help you write short definitions for these words, all of which occur in the passages above:

1. tolling
2. clogged
3. mesmerize
4. disinterested
5. euphoria
6. flux
7. satiated
8. resolute
9. console
10. masquerade
11. courted
12. lineal
13. cankering
14. tipple
15. hermitage

>> Task 1.9

Check that you can spell all the words you have worked on for Tasks 1.7 and 1.8. Test yourself or work with a partner and test each other. You should aim to get them 100% right – even if you have to relearn and retest several times.

Note: Brian Keenan and his publisher use the American spelling of mesmerize which is more usually spelled mesmerise in books published in Britain – although this is not something dictionaries, teachers (and computer spell checkers!) are very definite about. Consider too the spelling of words like realise and recognise. The best rule is probably to be consistent. So do not change your mind halfway through a piece of writing.

NUTS AND BOLTS

The sentence is the basic building block of most writing except poetry.

Sentences can take many forms. They should contain:
- an upper case (capital) letter at the beginning
- a full stop at the end (possibly incorporated into a question or exclamation mark)
- a subject
- at least one main verb
- an object (sometimes)
- other punctuation marks – such as commas – within the boundaries of the sentence (sometimes)
- other phrases and clauses (sometimes).

For example:

She had encountered that sort of behaviour, amongst the Jewesses, at other prisons.

The moment dwindles and dims like a dying fire.

subject
verb
object
extra phrases

Get into the habit of thinking of sentences as structures with fixed boundaries. They never end with commas.

Commas – and semi-colons – are weaker marks than the full stop. They are never used to end sentences – only within sentences.

The so-called 'run on comma' – a series of short sentences separated by commas – is **always** wrong.

For instance, this is incorrect:

> 'Too many people go to prison, crime rates are high.'

It should, of course, read:

> 'Too many people go to prison. Crime rates are high.'

➤➤ Task 1.10

Build each of these series of short sentences into one longer sentence, remembering the rules explained above:

1. Sarah Waters's book was published in 1999. I have read it three times.

2. Brian Keenan was held prisoner with John McCarthy. McCarthy is a journalist. Keenan is a university teacher.

3. 'The Prisoner of Chillon' is a long poem. It is by Lord Byron. Byron also wrote 'Don Juan'.

4. Oscar Wilde spent many hours on the treadmill in prison. He was a writer. He was used to being looked after. The treadmill broke his health.

5. Most people know little about Richard Lovelace. They know only two lines of his poetry. He led an interesting life. He lived in troubled times.

6. Britain has high prison numbers. It has more prisoners than most other European countries. Is this because it is better at catching criminals?

Once they have learned the rules of sentence structure, experienced, skilled writers often deliberately break them in order to achieve particular effects in their writing. Perhaps they want to suggest fear, hurry, panic or despair. They may intend the writing to 'sound' like thoughts or casual conversations rather than formal writing. Perhaps the aim is to make the reader laugh or to shock. The possible effects of writing styles are almost limitless.

The important thing for you at the moment is to learn the rules very thoroughly and get plenty of practice in applying them before you experiment with breaking them. You should also study the writing of professionals. Make yourself fully aware of the difference between mistakes and rule-breaking for effect.

➤➤ Task 1.11

Look very closely at this section of the extract from *An Evil Cradling*.

> I cannot. I will not eat this fruit. I sit in quiet joy, so complete, beyond the meaning of joy. My soul finds its own completeness in that bowl of colour. The forms of each fruit. The shape and curl and bend all so rich, so perfect. I want to bow before it. Loving that blazing, roaring, orange colour … Everything meeting in a moment of colour and form, my rapture no longer abstract euphoria.

• Study each sentence. Notice where Keenan uses conventional sentence structure and where he doesn't.

• Make notes and/or discuss it with a partner.

>> Task 1.11 (cont.)

- What effects is Keenan trying to achieve here?
- How far do you think he succeeds?
- What difference would it have made if he had used formal sentences throughout?

I/you/he/she/it/we/they could have been …

Could have here is a verb. It is the conditional past tense of the verb to have.

In spoken English, of course, it is usually contracted (elided) to could've.

And that's where the problem sometimes starts because the 've sounds a bit like 'of' which is a preposition (*The Merchant of Venice*, pint **of** milk, a man **of** few words, **of** course and so on).

So people sometimes make a mistake with it in writing (and even in speech).

Remember that have (or 've) nearly always comes after could. 'Could of' does not exist.

>> Task 1.12

Work with a partner. Take it in turns to dictate this paragraph to each other. Then check your work with this book to make sure you have it right.

Brian Keenan, prisoner of a minority Muslim group, is an example of great courage. He could have gone to pieces and infuriated his captors. Instead he thought of what he would do when he was released. He and John McCarthy, for example, planned an exploration of Patagonia which, years later, they were able to do together. He could have been killed in captivity as many hostages have been.

More speaking and listening activities

Read one or more of the books listed in the 'Wide Range Reading' section of this chapter. Present your thoughts about it to the class or a small group in the form of a two or three minute oral book review.

Organise a class or small group discussion or debate about any aspect of imprisonment which interests you.

Work with a partner. Take it in turns to read aloud a paragraph or so from one of the books recommended in the 'Wide Range Reading' section of this chapter. The person who is listening then summarises what he or she has heard for a third person. This works well if two pairs work side by side (but not within hearing distance) and all four read aloud a different passage.

Work with a partner. Create a role play based on the experience of two of the prisoners in 'Reading Gaol' as Oscar Wilde conveys it.

This puzzle is a bookish elimination. The answer to each clue is two words in the list. Once you have eliminated the answers to all 12 clues you will have one word left. This is the answer to the puzzle. If you get stuck, a reference book such as *The Oxford Companion to English Literature*, edited by Margaret Drabble, will help you.

Bleak   Harry   Henry   Hawk   Uncle   Farm   Romola   Anne   Bridget   Kim   Roosting
Jane   Beatrix   Tom   Blackbird   Animal   Joyce   Macavity   Branwell   Hamlet   Cymbeline
Marner   Jennie   Macbeth   Emma

1. Two by Shakespeare
2. Novel by George Orwell
3. Two girls as titles
4. Two houses
5. Two cats
6. Two named Jones
7. Two called Silas
8. Two named James
9. Two boys as titles
10. Two bookish Potters
11. Two Brontës
12. Poem by Ted Hughes

WIDE RANGE READING

These warmly recommended books all relate to the theme of imprisonment or to the writers mentioned in this chapter.

Fingersmith by Sarah Waters (2002). A marvellously exciting story of trickery and crime set in the 19th century from the author of *Affinity*. There is a section in which a character is imprisoned in a terrible Victorian 'lunatic asylum'. A real page turner which has also been serialised for television and is available on DVD. Try reading the book and then watching the DVD to see how well you think it is done.

The Collector by John Fowles (1963) is a novel about a solitary and strange young man with an obsession. He wants to 'collect' and imprison a young woman in his specially prepared cellar as if she were a butterfly. Her reactions, feelings and fears are beautifully done.

Oscar Wilde by Richard Ellmann (1988). This very readable biography is an excellent read for anyone who wants to know more about Wilde's life writing, marriage, and trial and the horrifying time he spent in prison. It seems remarkable now that the British justice system only just over a century ago was still putting some prisoners on treadmills for many hours a day.

Some Other Rainbow by John McCarthy and Jill Morrell (1993). During John McCarthy's long incarceration in Beirut his friend Jill Morrell led a big campaign to remind people all over the world of Mr McCarthy's plight. When he was eventually released they wrote *Some Other Rainbow* together describing everything that had happened from both points of view. Later the couple went their separate ways.

Taken on Trust by Terry Waite (1993). Terry Waite was special envoy to the Archbishop of Canterbury when he was taken hostage by militants in Beirut and held for several years with Brian Keenan, John McCarthy and two Americans. *Taken on Trust* is his – very interesting – account of what happened. It would be a good idea to read it along with *Some Other Rainbow* and *An Evil Cradling* because all three describe the same experience from very different angles and in different styles. Mr Keenan's is the most literary, but make up your own mind which account you admire the most and why.

A Long Walk to Freedom by Nelson Mandela (1995). Nelson Mandela was imprisoned in South Africa for 28 years during the white rule which insisted that blacks and whites be ruthlessly segregated. Mr Mandela fought for equality. He eventually became the elected President of a very different South Africa after his release. *A Long Walk to Freedom* is his deeply moving (and best selling) autobiography.

Great Expectations by Charles Dickens (1861). One of Dickens's greatest novels, *Great Expectations* famously opens with a terrified child being confronted by a fearsome escaped convict in a lonely churchyard. Much later comes a sad, but inevitable, long farewell in a London prison. In between, Dickens gives us a splendid plot full of colourful characters such as Miss Haversham, Wemmick and Joe Gargery.

Gulag Archipelago by Aleksandr Isanevich Solzhenitzyn (1973). This is a Russian novelist's famous account – written in exile – of being imprisoned in a remote region of Communist Russia mainly because he had liberal views and wrote books of which the authorities did not approve.

Al Capone Does my Shirts by Gennifer Choldenko (2004). Written specifically for teenagers this is the story of the family of one of the guards at Alcatraz where the notorious Al Capone was a prisoner in the 1930s. Alcatraz is a (real) island near San Francisco and each day the children cross by ferry to the city for school. Prisoners in Alcatraz have to help with community chores – hence the unlikely title of this entertaining and thoughtful novel. Today Alcatraz is a museum.

I am David by Anne Holm (1965). Also originally written for young readers this exquisite classic tale tells the story of a boy who escapes from a mid-20th century prison in southern Europe and – against all the odds – makes his way to the safety of Denmark. Like many a book based on a long and difficult journey or quest, *I am David* has a lasting epic quality.

MOVING ON

- **Find out about the work of the Howard League in British prisons today.**
- **Research the history and work of the charity Amnesty International which works to ease the plight of political prisoners all over the world.**
- **Elizabeth Fry (1780–1845) was an early prison reformer – see the back of a British £5 note for a picture of her. She was particularly concerned about the treatment of women (and their children) in prison. Read an account of her life and work.**

READY FOR A REAL CHALLENGE?

Read *Pilgrim's Progress* by John Bunyan (1628–1688). One of the great classics in English, it was published in two parts in 1678 and 1684. The deeply Christian author was in prison for many years (read up the history of the period to find out why) and wrote most of his finest work while he was behind bars. An alternative (or additional activity) would be to listen to *Pilgrim's Progress* as an audio book because the language is very powerful. There are several versions including a fine one read by Sir John Gielgud.

Have you ever been inside a mine? Most British coalmines are now closed but there are some good museums which allow you to experience how it would have felt to be miner – at Beamish near Durham in England or at Big Pit in Blaenafon in Wales, for example. In the early 19th century children as young as five were often forced to work long hours in coalmines until campaigners eventually got it stopped – worth thinking about as you read about various aspects of mining in this chapter. Can you work out why small children were so useful to mine owners?

It isn't just coal which is mined. Tin, gold, diamonds and many other metals and minerals have to be hacked from deep in the ground as some of the passages here show.

Read the three passages below. Then do the written tasks which follow each one.

Passage A

1

In Émile Zola's best novel we share the harrowing experiences of a downtrodden mining family in 19th century France.

5
The author was not himself a miner but, like Étienne in the novel, he spent many months with miners finding out at first hand about their lives. It's an intensely

10
gripping story. When I first read Germinal it kept me awake until 2am because I simply had to read on to find out what happened at the end. Here a group of

15
miners is at work.

The four colliers had spread themselves out, one above the other, to cover the whole coal-face. Each one occupied about four metres of the seam, and there were hooked planks between them to catch the coal as it fell. The seam was so thin, hardly more than fifty centimetres through at this point, that they were flattened between roof and wall, dragging themselves along by their elbows, unable to turn without grazing their shoulders. In order to get at the coal they had to lie on one side with twisted neck, arms above their heads, and wield their short-handled picks slantways.

20
Zacharie was at the bottom, with Lavaque and Chaval above him and Maheu at the top. Each cut into the bed of shale with his pick, then made two vertical slots in the coal and finally drove an iron wedge in at the top, thus loosening a block. The coal was soft, and in its fall broke up and rolled in pieces all over the men's stomachs and thighs. When these pieces, stopped by the planks, had collected beneath them, the

25
men disappeared, immured in the narrow cleft.

Maheu had the worst of it. At the top the temperature went up to 95 degrees (35 degrees Centigrade), air could not circulate, and he was stifled to death. In order to see he had to hang his lamp on a nail so near the top of his head that its heat set his

blood on fire. But it was the wet that really tortured him, for the rock, only a few
centimetres above his face, incessantly dripped fast and heavy drops with maddening
regularity always on the same spot. Try as he might to twist his neck and bend his
head backwards, the drops splashed relentlessly on his face, pit-a-pat. In a quarter of
an hour he was soaked through, what with his own sweat as well, and steaming like
a wash-tub.

On this particular morning he was swearing because a drop was determined to go in
his eye. He would not stop cutting, and the violent blows of his pick shook him, as he
lay between the two rocks like a fly caught between the pages of a book, in danger
of being flattened out.

Not a word was exchanged. They all hacked away, and all that could be heard was
their irregular tapping, which sounded distant and muffled, for in this dead air
sounds raised no echo but took on a harsh sonority. The darkness was mysterious in
its blackness, thick with flying coal-dust and heavy with gases which pressed down
upon the eyes. Only reddish points of light could be seen through the gauze covers
of the lamps. The coal face was barely discernible; it went up slantwise like a broad,
flat, sloping chimney, blackened with the impenetrable night of ten winters of soot,
and in it ghostly forms moved about and an occasional gleam threw into momentary
relief the shape of a man's haunch, a sinewy arm, a wild, dirty, criminal-looking face.
Now and then blocks of coal shimmered as they came loose, their surfaces or edges
glinted suddenly like crystal, and then all went black again, the picks tapped on

Etching of Bradley coal mine, near Bilston, 1880s

50 dully, and the only other sounds were panting breath and groans of discomfort and fatigue in the heavy air and dripping water.

Zacharie had been out on a spree the day before and was not feeling strong in the arm. He soon gave up work, finding the excuse that some timbering needed doing. This gave him a chance to go off into a dream, whistling to himself and staring 55 vaguely into space. Nearly three metres of the seam were cut away behind them, and they had not taken the precaution to prop up the rock. Fear of losing precious time made them heedless of danger.

'Here, you, the toff!' he called to Étienne. 'Pass me some wood.'

Étienne was being taught by Catherine how to wield his shovel, but he had to take 60 some wood along. There was a little store left over from the previous day. Usually pieces of wood ready cut to the size of the seam were sent down every morning.

'Look sharp, you lazy devil!' Zacharie went on, watching the new haulage man clumsily hoisting himself up amid the coal, with his arms encumbered by four pieces of oak.

65 With his pick he nicked a hole in the roof and another in the wall, ramming in the ends of the wood which thus propped up the rock. Every afternoon the rippers cleared away the waste after the colliers and filled in the cavities in the seam, leaving the timbering covered in. Only the top and bottom galleries were left intact for haulage.

From *Germinal* by Émile Zola (1885). Translated by Leonard Tanock (Penguin, 1954)

▸▸ Task 2.1

1. Why are conditions particularly difficult for Maheu?

2. What do you deduce from the passage about (a) Étienne and (b) Zacharie?

3. Summarise underground working conditions in this 19th century French mine. Use your own words but weave short quotations from the passage, marked off by inverted commas, into your sentences.

4. Look carefully at the way Zola, and his translator, describes the scene – the vocabulary, sentence shape and choice of image. What does this add to the overall impression of the passage? Answer in as much detail as you can.

Passage B

DH Lawrence was the son of a Nottinghamshire coal miner although he attended a grammar school and took a clerical job before becoming a teacher and writer. Several of his novels and short stories have mining as their setting because it was a world Lawrence knew well. He has a masterly understanding of the tensions and anxieties which miners and their families face every day. In this short story a family has been anxiously waiting for news of Walter. He should have been home from the mine hours ago.

It was half-past ten, and the old woman was saying: 'But it's trouble from beginning to end; you're never too old for trouble, never too old for that …' when the gate banged back, and there were heavy feet on the steps.

'I'll go, Lizzie, let me go', cried the old woman, rising. But Elizabeth was at the door. It was a man in pit-clothes.

'They're bringin' 'im, Missis', he said. Elizabeth's heart halted a moment. Then it surged on again, almost suffocating her.

'Is he – is it bad?' she asked.

The man turned away, looking at the darkness: 'The doctor says 'e'd been dead hours. 'E saw 'im i' th' lamp-cabin.'

The old woman, who stood just behind Elizabeth, dropped into a chair, and folded her hands, crying: 'Oh, my boy, my boy!'

'Hush!' said Elizabeth, with a sharp twitch of a frown. 'Be still, mother, don't waken the children: I wouldn't have them down for anything!'

The old woman moaned softly, rocking herself. The man was drawing away. Elizabeth took a step forward.

'How was it?' she asked.

'Well, I couldn't say for sure', the man replied, very ill at ease. ''E wor finishin' a stint an' the butties 'ad gone, an' a lot o' stuff came down atop 'im.'

'And crushed him?' cried the widow, with a shudder.

'No', said the man, 'it fell at th' back of 'im. 'E wor under th' face, and it niver touched 'im. It shut 'im in. It seems 'e wor smothered!'

Elizabeth shrank back. She heard the old woman behind her cry: 'What? … what did he say it was?'

The man replied more loudly: ''E wor smothered!'

Then the old woman wailed aloud, and this relieved Elizabeth.

35 'Oh mother', she said, putting her hand on the old woman, 'don't waken the children, don't waken the children.'

She wept a little, unknowing, while the old mother rocked herself and moaned. Elizabeth remembered that they were bringing him home, and she must be ready. 'They'll lay him in the parlour', she said to herself, standing a moment pale and
40 perplexed.

'You'll have to move from there, mother', said Elizabeth. 'They'll be bringing him in. Come in the rocker.'

The old mother rose mechanically, and seated herself by the fire, continuing to lament. Elizabeth went into the pantry for another candle, and there, in the little
45 penthouse under the naked tiles, she heard them coming. She stood in the pantry doorway, listening. She heard them pass down the three steps, a jumble of shuffling footsteps and muttering voices. The old woman was silent. The men were in the yard.

Then Elizabeth heard Matthews, the manager of the pit, say 'You go first, Jim. Mind!'

The door came open, and the two women saw a collier backing into the room, holding
50 one end of a stretcher, on which they could see the nailed pit-boots of the dead man. The two carriers halted, the man at the head stooping to the lintel of the door.

'Wheer will you have him?' asked the manager, a short, white-bearded man.

'In the parlour', she said.

'In there Jim!' pointed the manager, and the carriers backed round into the tiny
55 room. The coat with which they had covered the body fell off as they awkwardly turned through the two doorways, and the women saw their man, naked to the waist, lying stripped for work.

From 'Odour of Chrysanthemums' a short story by DH Lawrence (1914)

>> Task 2.2

1. One woman has lost her husband, the other her son. How do their reactions differ? Answer in your own words but refer very closely to the passage.

2a. What impression does DH Lawrence give you of the atmosphere in and around this traditional miner's cottage and how does he achieve it? Look carefully at the detail of what is inside the house and at the sounds from outside.

b. Why do you think the story is called 'Odour of Chrysanthemums'? Make your answer as full as you can.

3. The old woman and the living miners speak in an old Nottinghamshire dialect with a strong accent. What do you think about this way of writing? In your answer you may find it helpful to consider the following:

• Why do you think Elizabeth speaks standard English?

• Does DH Lawrence's method of writing it work for you as a reader?

• Explain your thoughts in as much detail as you can.

1

Passage C

In 2006 millions of people followed the story of two men who were trapped in their workplace – a gold mine at Beaconsfield in Tasmania, Australia. This is an account – from a British national daily newspaper – of the miners' final rescue.

5

10

Two Tasmanian gold miners trapped 3,000 feet underground for 14 days were rescued yesterday, ending a saga that had gripped Australia. The rescue of the pair, who had been feared dead, has been described as 'an inspiring example of Australian mateship.'

Todd Russell, 34, and Brant Webb, 37, were trapped in a safety cage in the mine in Beaconsfield, Tasmania, after a 2.1 magnitude earthquake caused a collapse of underground rocks and killed their colleague, 44-year-old Larry Knight on April 25. Initially, it was feared that the two men, both married and both with three children, had also perished but investigators using a thermal imaging camera five days after the collapse found them still alive and the non-stop effort to bring the pair to safety began.

15

The men were able to walk unaided from the mine's main lift shaft, despite their ordeal and cramped muscles. They hugged family and friends before climbing into two ambulances.

20

A fire engine drove through the town with its siren wailing to alert locals to news that the pair had been rescued. A church bell rang out in celebration shortly after 5am (1900 GMT).

Hundreds of locals from the close-knit town of Beaconsfield, in the island state of Tasmania, gathered at the gates of the mine to welcome the men, who have become national heroes. Television cameras, photographers and journalists shouting questions also greeted the men above ground, reflecting the enormous media encampment that had followed every twist of the rescue effort.

Television networks, whose bulletins had already been interrupting normal television programming, cut live to the news that the men had been saved.

The miners received medical treatment before appearing in front of members of the public. Onlookers applauded as an ambulance carrying the men drove slowly past with its doors open.

The men appeared to be in good health and smiled broadly, punching the air in jubilation and waving to wellwishers. 'The great escape is over', union official Bill Shorten told Nine Network television after the men emerged. 'A giant rock of pressure has been taken off these families.' Mine manager Matthew Gill, who is a close friend of the pair, said the men were 'incredible people', adding: 'I am amazed at their condition.'

He said the rescue operation had involved keeping the miners horizontal for as long as possible in case they were injured. The men were then pulled to safety through a vertical tunnel.

But there was a bittersweet edge to the rescue, as it came just hours before the funeral of their colleague Mr Knight. The father-of-four is due to be buried in Launceston today. Mr Gill said the two survivors had expressed a desire to attend the service.

The men had displayed an impressively laid-back attitude to their fate throughout their ordeal. They survived the first week on a cereal bar and by licking the water from the rocks but have since been fed on meals passed down to them through a 40ft pipe.

On a psychologist's advice, an iPod with their favourite music stored on it was also sent through the pipe to keep up their spirits.

Yesterday, according to the local Mercury newspaper, they made an unsuccessful request for chips and gravy to be sent down but doctors would only agree to chicken and cheese bread rolls with some tinned fruit for dessert. Omelettes and home-made soups were also dispatched through a device similar to a dumb waiter.

The trapped men also joked about asking for the classified ads column from the local paper so that they could see what other jobs might be on offer.

The bonhomie which characterised the rescue attempt was saluted by the Australian Prime Minister, John Howard. 'It's just been terrific to see the way that community has worked together, the mayor, the churches, the union leaders, all of them have come together, emergency workers and, most importantly, all those who have actually gone down and dug through to try and rescue their mates', he said.

The Mercury reported that the Prime Minister had hailed the saga as 'an example of Australian mateship'.

The rescue team worked around the clock, using low-impact explosives, hydraulic rock splitters, hand-held drills and diamond-tipped chainsaws.

They faced enormous problems in trying to drill their way in zigzag fashion through the rock without endangering the lives of the men as they tried to cut them a metre-wide escape tunnel in the 25 degree underground heat.

The two men had to help their rescuers by spreading grout over loose rocks to prevent collapses around them as the final push was made in an area where gold had been discovered in 1877.

As the rescuers appeared to be getting closer, excitement mounted.

'The fat lady might not have sung but I can certainly hear her clearing her vocal cords', Mr Shorten, national secretary of the Australian Workers Union, told the Associated Press shortly before the men emerged.

There was further drama when one of Australia's best-known journalists, Richard Carleton, collapsed and died during a press conference about the rescue attempts. Carleton, 62, of Nine Network's 60 Minutes programme, had just asked the mine manager about the company's safety record when he suffered a heart attack.

His report, which aired after his death, was critical of safety procedures at the mine.

Journalists covering the rescue attempt found themselves suddenly reporting on the death of one of their colleagues, a man who had covered many of the major foreign stories of the past four decades and who had worked for ABC and the BBC in a long, award-strewn and sometimes controversial career. Mr Howard described him as 'a colourful bloke'.

Carleton had famously crossed swords with Bob Hawke, one of Mr Howard's predecessors.

From *The Guardian*, Tuesday, 9th May 2006. Written by Duncan Campbell, Alex Kumi and agencies.

❯❯ Task 2.3

1. Summarise what the trapped men and their rescuers did during the 14-day ordeal to stop Todd Russell and Brant Webb from losing hope. Write in as much detail as you can using your own words with short quotations from the passage.

2. Describe the problems which faced the rescuers.

3. Remember this is a news story from a national daily newspaper, published in Britain – a long way from Tasmania. Comment on the way the story unfolds. In your answer it may help you to:

   • Look carefully at the opening paragraph.

   • Then consider the repetition, short sentences and brief paragraphs in the rest of the story.

   • Work out why certain people are quoted.

   • Decide how useful you think their words are – do they add anything to the story?

   • Say whether you think anything valuable would have been lost if the last four paragraphs had been omitted.

Passage D

Norman Nicholson (1914-1987) was a fine poet who came from Millom in Cumbria and often wrote about his home area. During his lifetime the local, formerly thriving, mining industry gradually closed down. Cleator Moor is a small industrial town on the west coast of Cumbria.

Cleator Moor

1 From one shaft at Cleator Moor
They mined for coal and ore.
This harvest below ground could show
Black and red currants on one tree.

5 In furnaces they burnt the coal,
The ore was smelted into steel,
And railway lines from end to end
Corseted the bulging land.

10 Pylons sprouted on the fells,
Stakes were driven in like nails,
And the ploughed fields of Devonshire
Were sliced with the steel of Cleator Moor

The land waxed fat and greedy too,
It would not share the fruits it grew,
15 And coal and ore, as sloe and plum,
Lay black and red for jamming time.

The pylons rusted on the fells,
The gutters leaked beside the walls,
And women searched the ebb-tide tracks
20 For knobs of coal or broken sticks.

But now the pits are wick* with men,
Digging like dogs dig for a bone:
For food and life we dig the earth—
In Cleator Moor the dig for death.

25 Every wagon of cold coal
Is fire to drive a turbine wheel;
Every knuckle of soft ore
A bullet in a soldier's ear.

The miner at the rockface stands,
30 With his segged† and bleeding hands
Heaps on his head the fiery coal,
And feels the iron in his soul.

'Cleator Moor' by Norman Nicholson (1944)

* 'Wick' is a northern England dialect
word meaning active or lively.
† Dialect word meaning blistered
and calloused.

Cleator Moor in 1905

South Crofty was a complex of mines (for tin and other metals) between Cambourne and Redruth in Cornwall dating back to the 16th century. Cornwall's last tin mine, it closed - controversially - in 1998, although part of it is now open for tourists. Tin was mined in Cornwall for thousands of years. Elsie Balme is a living poet based in Cornwall. This poignant sonnet is deeply moving.

Sonnet for South Crofty

1　If words were rocks, I'd hew them from the ground
　And smelt a song of Crofty from their ore,
　So strong grown men might weep to hear the sound
　Of the great mine that was—and is no more.

5　The long inheritance—three thousand years
　Is ended by the scratching of a pen—
　As jobless men trudge homeward with their fears,
　As mundic* turns the river red again.

　Red with the mine's blood—Crofty's bled to death
10　Time gone, day done, the story on the page
　All told and over swifter than the breath
　Of wind that rattles in that empty cage.

　Sleep soft, South Crofty, pass into dreams, old friend.
　Cornwall shall honour you until time's end.

'Sonnet for South Crofty' by Elsie Balme (exact date unknown)

* 'Mundic' is the old Cornish word for iron pyrites, a yellowish metal known as 'fool's gold'. The waste from tin mines contained a lot of it.

>> Task 2.4

1a. What does Norman Nicholson mean in Passage D by the 'harvest below ground' (line 3)? How well do you think this image works?

 b. Explain and comment on the words 'And the ploughed fields of Devonshire/ Were sliced with the steel of Cleator Moor.'

2. What makes the mine at 'Cleator Moor' 'wick' again? How do you know?

3. Comment on the mood of 'Sonnet for South Crofty' in Passage E. What feelings does Elsie Balme want to convey? Use short quotations (using inverted commas) from the poem to illustrate your answer.

4. What are the characteristics of Elsie Balme's poem which make it a sonnet? How does the form of the poem add to its meaning and effectiveness?

5. Pick out and comment on two or three words, phrases or ideas which you find interesting from each poem.

6. Which of the two poems do you prefer? Work out your choice and explain your reasons. It may help you to formulate your thoughts if you discuss your ideas with a partner before you begin to write.

Writing about literature

Study this example of literary criticism on the 'Odour of Chrysanthemums' as an example of how you might write about prose.

> Lawrence's use of short sentences and simple vocabulary in the paragraph which begins 'Then she lighted a candle' adds to the numb horror of the moment as Elizabeth sets about the practical things she has to do before the men bring her husband's body home. The opening sentence, for example, is a basic compound in which two statements are linked by the conjunction 'and'. Only two of its 11 words have more than one syllable. The third sentence has a similar structure. This conveys a strong sense of her clinging grimly to practicalities. The chilling adjectives ('cold', 'damp', 'deathly') add to this effect. So do the onomatopoeic verbs 'shivered' and 'moaning'. The whole paragraph is written with intense sensuousness. Sounds (the mother-in-law), sights (the appearance of the room), smells (the flowers), sensations (the cold) are all evoked. Against this there is homely vocabulary such as 'bit of carpet' and the clean shirt 'at the fire to air' to remind the reader that Elizabeth is an ordinary housewife.

>> Task 2.5

Choose a paragraph from one of the prose passages in this chapter. Comment on it in detail as the writer has above.

Personal Writing

>> Task 2.6

1. Imagine you are a modern health and safety inspector. You have visited the mine described in Passage A. Write your report setting out how working conditions should be improved.

2. Write a diary entry by Mr Matthews, the pit (mine) manager, describing from his point of view the events on the day when Elizabeth's husband died (in 'Odour of Chrysanthemums').

3. Imagine you are a journalist. Write a news story, modelled on Passage C about (a) the French mine in *Germinal* or (b) the death of Elizabeth's husband in 'Odour of Chrysanthemums'.

4. Write a poem about something or someone which/who is no longer there. Use 'Cleator Moor' or 'Sonnet for South Crofty' as a model or write the poem in any style you wish.

5. Write a story in which mining plays an important part.

6. Write about mining in any way you wish.

Writing tip

Vary the length of your sentences. A piece of writing in which all the sentences are roughly the same length is usually dull and flat.

Look at this example from 'Odour of Chrysanthemums':

> The old mother rose mechanically, and seated herself by the fire, continuing to lament. Elizabeth went into the pantry for another candle, and there, in the little penthouse under the naked tiles, she heard them coming. She stood in the pantry doorway, listening. She heard them pass down the three steps, a jumble of shuffling footsteps and muttering voices. The old woman was silent. The men were in the yard.

In one paragraph DH Lawrence has a sequence of sentences which have – in order – 14, 22, 7, 16, 5 and 6 words. Read it aloud. You will notice that varied sentence length creates rhythm which matters as much in prose as in poetry.

A useful technique is sometimes to build a paragraph of three sentences, each one shorter than the one before. It is quite dramatic and makes your reader want to hurry on to the next paragraph. Finishing a paragraph with a short sentence can be dramatic.

Émile Zola uses the word **immured**. It comes from the Latin word *murus* – a wall. It means **walled up** or **imprisoned**.

We also derive several English words from the Latin nouns *domus* – a house and *veritas* – truth.

>> Task 2.7

Write definitions for the following:

1. mural	5. verify
2. veracity	6. transmural
3. domestic	7. domicile
4. extramural study	8. domain

There is a **chiffonier** in the parlour described in 'Odour of Chrysanthemums'. This was **a small sideboard with shelves or drawers**. Although fashions change with every generation, whenever furniture was made nearly every piece was to:

put things on
put things in
sit or lie on

Some items (think of a piano stool with a box for music or the modern 'captain' bunk bed which incorporates a desk and clothes storage) combine two of more of these functions.

Novels, poems and plays written in the past often refer to items of furniture which may no longer be familiar.

>> Task 2.8

Find out what each of the following pieces of furniture were (or are) and make brief notes on each:

1. Chesterfield
2. Tallboy
3. Secretaire
4. Settle

5. Canterbury
6. Whatnot
7. Credenza
8. Davenport

>> Task 2.9

The answer to each of the following 'clues' is a word from one of the passages in this chapter. Take great care with spelling because these words are often misspelt. Write out several times any word which gives you problems.

1. went out of sight: d …
2. device for measuring heat: t …
3. without stopping: i …
4. from time to time: o …
5. evident: d …
6. hard red wood: m …

7. miner: c …
8. clumsily: a …
9. got: r …
10. made furrows in land: p …
11. expert on the human mind: p …
12. short up-to-date report: b …

NUTS AND BOLTS

It is useful to understand the classes into which words fall. You will almost certainly have learned about these word classes – sometimes known as the 'parts of speech' – many times before. You will write better, and be more skilled at analysing and discussing how writers get their effects, if you have a confident map of this information firmly in your head.

Remember that the same word can belong to several different word classes according to the way in which it is being used. Or – to put it another way – words are very adaptable and can do more than one job.

Is she in the top **set** for maths? (noun)

The surgeon **set** my sister's broken femur so it is as good as new. (verb)

We all held our breath because the tennis match had reached **set** point. (adjective)

She is **as** dark-haired as her sister. (adverb)

We must go to the bank **as** we have very little cash. (conjunction – meaning 'because')

As Luke's friend, I thought I would accompany him to the headmaster's office. (preposition)

Another problem is that experts do not always agree about the details of word classes – and they tend to have very strong views.

>> Task 2.10

Write at least three sentences using each of these words in a different word class. Write in brackets after each one what class it is in your sentence.

1.	after	5.	pass
2.	space	6.	book
3.	type	7.	up
4.	through	8.	over

>> Task 2.11

What part of speech – or word class – do you think the words in **bold** are in the sentences below? Given the differences in opinion among experts there is more than one possible answer to each. You might find it helpful to discuss your thoughts with a partner before you decide on your answers.

1. This is **your** pen and that is **mine**.

2. The bank agreed to write **off** the man's debt.

3. This belt is **the** fashion item to have this year.

4. **Galloping** inflation affects many countries.

5. **Those** statistics are flawed.

6. **Our** house is haunted.

NUTS AND BOLTS

'Redundancy' is a good example of a word which changes its meaning quite drastically according to context. In industry it means job loss because a person is no longer needed in the workplace. When referring to language it means the use of unnecessary words.

In spoken and colloquial English we use a large number of phrasal verbs – verbs joined to a not strictly necessary adverb or preposition for emphasis. Thus we tend to 'sit down' instead of 'sit', 'meet up' instead of 'meet', and 'print out' instead of 'print'. Make a list of phrasal verbs, e.g. stand up, stand down, stand out, stand against and so on. There are hundreds – and they tend to cause learners of English as a second language many headaches.

In writing when you want to be precise and brief – perhaps in a factual report – they are best avoided. Get into the habit of editing your work and deleting all redundant words – often parts of phrasal verbs.

Make sure you also avoid tautology, sometimes known as pleonasm – the use of two or more words which mean the same thing. Don't write for example: 'She died in a fatal accident.' If it was fatal then of course she died. Write either: 'She died in an accident.' or 'Her accident was fatal.'

≫ Task 2.12

Rewrite this 76-word passage deleting all redundancy. How few words can you reduce it to?

> They all agreed and unanimously decided to go on a walking tour on foot from their homes in Newcastle and around Northumberland and then back to Newcastle where they lived. But they argued and strongly disagreed about their itinerary and particularly what route they should take. Should they stick to tarmac lanes or should they amble slowly and in a leisurely way on footpaths appreciating the countryside and the beauties of the scenery at their leisure?

GET IT RIGHT

This sentence, written by the newspaper's banking correspondent, Philip Aldrick, appeared in *The Daily Telegraph* on 14th September 2007:

> Some banks raise most of their money from the likes of you and I – in retail deposits such as current or savings accounts.

It is grammatically wrong. Mr Aldrick should have written 'you and me'.

There are two ways of understanding why.

First learn that 'I' should be used only as the subject of a verb and 'me' as a direct or indirect object. In Mr Aldrick's sentence 'I' is not the subject. He is using an indirect object of 'from … me' so 'me' is correct.

Alternatively try this, or any other similar sentence which is giving you problems: remove the words between the verb and the pronoun. Mr Aldrick would not have written or said: 'Banks raise money from I.' He (or you) would have said 'Banks raise money from me.' The grammar remains the same even when other words come between the verb and the pronoun.

Study these examples which are all correct. Learn them by heart as examples of correct use if it helps.

- Goodbye from my brother and me.

- Can you give Polly and me some help, please?

- It was I who raised the alarm.

- Jonathan, Deepa, May-Kim and I are all waiting for our marks.

- She and I are cross.

Sadly, you will often see this error – even in quality newspapers which should have been better edited. Training yourself to spot the mistake, and mentally correcting it, is a good way of strengthening your own grasp of this point.

>> Task 2.13

Write six sentences using 'I' and 'me' in as many varied ways as you can to reinforce your learning.

Words which sound, or look, similar or the same are often confused although they have completely different meanings. Do not confuse, for example, **ingenious** and **ingenuous** or **official** with **officious**. Check the meaning of those words now if you're not sure and then tackle Task 2.14 over the page.

>> Task 2.14

Use each of the following pairs of words in two separate sentences to show the difference in meaning. Use a dictionary to help you.

1. flaunt/flout

2. counsellor/councillor

3. fictional/fictitious

4. uninterested/disinterested

5. stationery/stationary

6. veracious/voracious (remember the work you did in Task 2.7 to help you with this one)

More speaking and listening activities

Prepare a performance for the rest of the class of one of the poems in this chapter. It will probably be better if you learn it by heart. Think very carefully about expression and pacing.

Work in a group of three. Take the roles of the two Tasmanian coal miners and a journalist conducting a television interview.

Work in a group of four. One of you plays the role of Étienne in the extract from *Germinal*. The other three question him about his experience and observation in the mine.

Organise a small group, or a classroom discussion, on ways of dealing with death in different cultures. Take what happens in 'Odour of Chrysanthemums' as your starting point.

Use a reference book or the internet to find the names of the novels which these authors published for the first time in the given year. Each title is a **single** word. The initial letters of the ten titles are an anagram of the title of a famous novel.

Joseph Conrad 1904
Elizabeth Gaskell 1853
AS Byatt 1990
Charlotte Brontë 1859
Samuel Butler 1972

Frederick Forsyth 1996
Benjamin Disraeli 1845
James Joyce 1922
Ian McEwan 2001
Virginia Woolf 1928

WIDE RANGE READING

All these books relate to some aspect of mining.

How Green was my Valley by Richard Llewellyn (1939). This novel is an engrossing family saga set in South Wales and describes all the horrors that mining can lead to, although there is happiness too. Eventually some characters emigrate to Patagonia in South America in search of a better life.

The Colour by Rose Tremain (2003). Set in New Zealand, *The Colour* is a gripping drama about sacrifice and greed during the mid-19th century gold rush. A couple from Norfolk cross the world to settle on South Island expecting to find gold and get rich – but it doesn't quite work out like that. Rose Tremain writes very graphically about the suffering characters go through in this fine novel.

Sons and Lovers by DH Lawrence (1913). This is Lawrence's most famous – and best – novel. It tells the compelling story of Paul Morel who grows up in a Nottinghamshire mining community and eventually moves away from it – and his mother. It is partly autobiographical. If you cannot imagine life in a miner's family you will after you've read this.

Hungry Hill by Daphne du Maurier (1943). A very satisfying family saga about tin miners in Cornwall. Several of Daphne Du Maurier's novels (*Rebecca*, for example) are set in Cornwall where the author lived and worked for most of her adult life. She is an outstanding storyteller and a skilled creator of atmosphere and tension.

Gold Mine by Wilbur Smith (1988). Try this thriller for a fast-paced read set in the cut-throat world of South Africa's gold mining industry. It isn't great literature, but you develop critical skills by reading widely and Wilbur Smith is a good storyteller who certainly ensures that you want to go on turning the pages.

Kit's Wilderness by David Almond (1999). Written specifically for older children and teenagers *Kit's Wilderness* is set in mining country in the north-east of England. It is a very visual novel with a strong sense of place. David Almond's terse style is ideally suited to showing how relationships are affected when things go wrong and it's a very moving book.

Annerton Pit by Peter Dickinson (1977). This novel for young adults tells the story of Jake whose parents are on holiday. Meanwhile his grandfather is roaming around Britain looking for ghosts and sending a postcard to Jake each week. When the postcards stop coming, Jake's brother buys a motorbike and they go north to look for an old man in the whispering maze of Annerton Pit, a place of dark and fear where something waits for Jake.

MOVING ON

- Most of Britain's coal mines closed in the 1980s and 1990s. Research the history of why this was, how people reacted and the effect of the closures. You might use what you discover as the basis for a presentation to the rest of the class.

- Read Zola's *Germinal*. Then see the 1993 film which is available on DVD. Directed by Gerard Berri, it is in French with English subtitles. Work out how satisfactory an interpretation of the book you think it is. If you do this with a partner you will have the advantage of someone to discuss your thoughts with.

- DH Lawrence was the son of a Nottinghamshire miner. Make a poster for the classroom wall about his life and work. Include a time-line and the titles of his main works. You could also make a map to show his worldwide travels and include a photograph of him – and anything else about him which interests you. The internet is probably your best resource for this.

READY FOR A REAL CHALLENGE?

Mining literature has become a small genre in its own right. Because so many people come from families where mining was once a way of life the experience is deep in our culture. Writing about mining communities is also a way of showing oppressed people fighting against their bosses – which appeals to many readers. Some people therefore say that most novels and poems about mining are political. Find out as much as you can about mining literature. Build a bibliography of novels and an anthology of poems about mining, miners and mines. Use libraries and the internet to help you. Read as widely as you can in this genre. Decide for yourself how far you would agree that most of it is political.

Most of us have been on the sea even if it was only for a short ferry trip. Some of you may also have been in yachts and perhaps helped to sail them. Or perhaps you've done some sea fishing? One way or another we all have some idea of how it feels to be in a vessel buffeted by the waves and many of us will have felt, or been, seasick.

People crossing water on modern stabilised ferries, or in well-equipped small boats, generally have it easy. Sea voyagers in the past – or those who travel in very different circumstances – had or have a very different experience of the sea as the colourful group of prose passages and poems which underpin this chapter show. Happy sailing!

Read the three passages below. Then do the written tasks which follow.

Passage A

1

Charles Dickens (1812-1870) is the world famous author of novels such as David

5 Copperfield and Nicholas Nickleby. He was also a good journalist and a fine travel writer. He first visited the USA in 1824 where he read aloud from his books and

10 was treated as a great celebrity. His – very interesting – book, American Notes, was published in 1842. It is often very critical of America and its people, many of

15 whom objected to the book. Here he describes part of his crossing of the Atlantic Ocean from Britain to the USA.

It is the third morning. I am awakened out of my sleep by a dismal shriek from my wife, who demands to know whether there's any danger. I rouse myself, and look out of bed. The water-jug is plunging and leaping like a lively dolphin; all the smaller articles are afloat, except my shoes, which are stranded on a carpet-bag, high and dry, like a couple of coal-barges. Suddenly I see them spring into the air, and behold the looking glass, which is nailed to the wall, sticking fast upon the ceiling. At the same time the door entirely disappears, and a new one is

20 opened in the floor. Then I begin to comprehend that the state-room is standing on its head.

Before it is possible to make any arrangement at all compatible with this state of things, the ship rights. Before one can say 'Thank Heaven!' she wrongs again. Before one can cry she *is* wrong, she seems to have started forward, and to be a creature

25 actively running of its own accord, with broken knees and failing legs, through every variety of hole and pitfall, and stumbling constantly. Before one can so much as wonder, she takes a high leap into the air. Before she has well done that, she takes a deep dive into the water. Before she has gained the surface, she throws a summerset.* The instant she is on her legs, she rushes backward. And so she goes on

30 staggering, heaving, wrestling, leaping, diving, jumping, pitching, throbbing, rolling
and rocking: and going through all these movements, sometimes by turns, and
sometimes all together: until one feels disposed to roar for mercy.

A steward passes. 'Steward!'

'Sir?'

35 'What *is* the matter? What *do* you call this?'

'Rather a heavy sea on, sir, and a head-wind.'

A head-wind! Imagine a human face upon the vessel's prow, with fifteen thousand
Samsons† intent on driving her back, and hitting her exactly between the eyes
whenever she attempts to advance an inch. Imagine the ship herself, with every pulse
40 and artery of her huge body swollen and bursting under this mal-treatment, sworn
to go on or die. Imagine the wind howling, the sea roaring, the rain beating: all in
furious array against her. Picture the sky both dark and wild, and the clouds, in
fearful sympathy with the waves, making another ocean in the air. Add to all this the
clattering on deck and down below; the tread of hurried feet; the loud hoarse shouts
45 of seamen; the gurgling in and out of water through the scuppers; with every now
and then, the striking of a heavy sea upon the planks above, with the deep, dead,
heavy sound of thunder heard within a vault; – and there's the head-wind of that
January morning.

I say nothing of what may be called the domestic noises of the ship: such as the
50 breaking of glass and crockery, the tumbling down of stewards, the gambols,
overhead, of loose casks and truant dozens of bottled porter, and the very
remarkable and far from exhilarating sounds raised in their various state-rooms by
the seventy passengers who were too ill to get up for breakfast. I say nothing of
them: although I lay listening to this concert for three or four days, I don't think I
55 heard it for more than a quarter of a minute, at the expiration of which term, I lay
down again, excessively sea-sick.

From *American Notes* by Charles Dickens (1842)

* an old form of *somersault*.
† refers to Samson, a strong man who fought and killed the Philistines in *The Bible* (Judges, 15).

> **>> Task 3.1**
>
> 1. Summarise briefly in your own words what is happening in this passage. Write no more than two sentences.
>
> ───────────────────────────────────────
>
> 2. What does Dickens mean by (a) the domestic noises of the ship (line 49) (b) far from exhilarating sounds (line 52)?
>
> ───────────────────────────────────────
>
> 3. Dickens compares the ship with 'a creature actively running of its own accord'. How does he develop this metaphor?
>
> ───────────────────────────────────────
>
> 4. Many people regard Dickens as a great comic writer. How effective do you find this passage as a piece of comic writing? You might like to consider:
>   • his metaphors
>   • his conversation with the steward
>   • his wife's reaction
>   • his last sentence.

Passage B

Thor Heyerdahl was a Norwegian scientist, intrigued by the history and movements of the human race. Ancient rock carvings in Polynesia reminded him of others in America. He became convinced that over a thousand years ago there were Pacific crossings in primitive vessels. It seemed unlikely and most experts dismissed the idea. So Heyerdahl, with a small group of men, set out to test his theory. They built a balsawood raft, named Kon-Tiki, and sailed it across the Pacific – in 1947 long before the days of mobile phones and satellite links. So there was no safety back-up. They succeeded and Heyerdahl's best-selling book describing the voyage was published the following year. This extract describes some of the wildlife they observed and ate.

1   After a week or so the water grew calmer, and we noticed that it became blue instead of green. We began to go west-north-west instead of due north-west, and took this as the first faint sign that we had got out of the coastal current and had some hope of being carried out to sea.

5 The very first day we were alone on the sea we had noticed fish round the raft, but were too much occupied with steering to think of fishing. The second day we went right into a shoal of
10 sardines, and soon afterwards an eight-foot blue shark came along and rolled over with its white belly uppermost as it rubbed against the raft's stern, where Herman and Bengt stood barelegged in
15 the seas steering. It played round us for a while, but disappeared when we got the hand harpoon ready for action.

The Kon-Tiki raft, 1947

Next day we were visited by tunnies, bonitos, and dolphins and when a big flying fish thudded on board we used it as bait and at once pulled in two large dolphins
20 (dorados) weighing from 20 to 35lb each. This was food for several days. On one steering watch we could see many fish we did not even know, and one day we came into a school of porpoises which seemed quite endless. The black backs tumbled about, packed close together, right in to the side of the raft, and sprang up here and there all over the sea as far as we could see from the masthead. And the nearer we
25 came to the equator, the farther from the coast, the commoner flying fish became. When at last we came out into the blue water where the sea rolled by majestically, sunlit and sedate, ruffled by gusts of wind we could see them glittering like a rain of projectiles, shooting from the water and flying in a straight line till their power of flight was exhausted and they vanished beneath the surface.

30 If we set the little paraffin lamp out at night flying fish were attracted by the light and, large and small, shot over the raft. They often struck the bamboo cabin or the sail and tumbled helplessly on the deck. For, unable to get a take-off by swimming through the water, they remained lying and kicking helplessly, like large red-eyed herrings with long breast fins. It sometimes happened that we heard an outburst of
35 strong language from a man on deck when a cold flying fish came unexpectedly at a good speed slap into his face. They always came at a good pace and snout first, and if they caught one full in the face they made it burn and tingle. But the unprovoked attack was quickly forgiven by the injured party, for this, with all its drawbacks, was a maritime land of enchantment where delicious fish dishes came hurtling through the
40 air. We used to fry them for breakfast, and whether it was the fish, the cook, or our appetites, they reminded us of fried troutlings once we had scraped the scales off.

The cook's first duty when he got up in the morning was to go out on deck and collect all the flying fish that had landed on board in the course of the night. There were usually half a dozen or more, and one morning we found twenty-six fat flying

45   fish on the raft. Knut was much upset one morning because, when he was standing operating with the frying pan, a flying fish struck him on the hand instead of landing right in the cooking fat.

From *The Kon-Tiki Expedition* by Thor Heyerdahl (1948)

Task 3.2

1. Summarise what you have learned about flying fish from this passage. Mention their behaviour, their appearance and their use to Heyerdahl and his crew.

2. What two factors seemed to affect the number of fish and other creatures around the raft? (Note: Porpoises are mammals.)

3. How does the shark differ from the porpoises and in what ways is it similar? You might like to think about the size, appearance, habits and motivation of the two animals. Use only the information you can deduce from the passage.

Passage C

Doris Lessing is an important and enjoyable novelist. She has won many top prizes for her novels and stories – some of which are set in Rhodesia (now Zimbabwe) where she grew up. In 2007 she was awarded the best prize of all: the Nobel Prize for Literature. This extract comes from one of four substantial short stories (sometimes known as novellas) in a book called The Grandmothers. It tells the tale of a British World War Two soldier travelling by sea to India and the relationship he has on the way. Here he and his comrades are experiencing the notorious Bay of Biscay off the west coast of France.

1   The Bay of Biscay was doing its worst. From top to bottom of the great ship the men were ill, and the smell anywhere below decks, or in the cabins, was foul.

In their hammocks the constant swaying, so bad that the hammock of one man knocking another could set off five in a row, was unendurable. Out of their

5   hammocks, trying to sit at the table, there was no relief. Up on deck, surrounded by

a grey tumult of water, was as bad. By the evening of the second day it was evident that this was a ship of the sick, except for a minority who were apparently immune, and who volunteered for mess duty, where they could eat as much as they liked, but were ordered for cleaning duty, which meant swabbing fouled cabins and fouler

10   decks.

Below the layer where B Platoon was, which they felt must be the ultimate hell-hole, was a deeper layer of crammed humanity. When the ship had been fitted out to take troops, attempts had been made at ventilating these depths, but in those commodious spaces, which had once housed the luggage of the rich, or foodstuffs

15   designed for peacetime menus, the air was bad and everyone was sick down there. On the third night men on E Deck heard screaming from below them: this was how they became aware they were not the lowest depths of suffering. Claustrophobia, they knew at once; for they themselves were in danger of breaking and screaming. It was not only the press of the ship's walls about them, but knowing how the great

20   dark outside went on to a horizon they knew must be there, but could not see: no moon, no stars, thick cloud, dark above and dark below.

On the fourth night, ignoring the corporal who followed them, not even expostulating, they were on deck, where at least the air blew cold. They lay along the walls of a deck, keeping their eyes shut, and endured. Rupert Fitch, the farmer's

25   son, was better off than most. He sat with back against a wall, his head upon his knees, and hummed dance tunes and hymns. The great ship ploughed on into the dark, with a deep steady swaying motion. In the morning nothing had changed, but the deck was crowded with men, some from the lower depths. Corporal Clark, the shepherd of B Platoon, was lying like them, rolling a little as the ship did, face down,

30   head on his arms.

There came tripping down the companionway Sergeant 'Ginger' Perkins, a short compact-bodied man, with bristly carroty hair, and a belligerent stance cultivated for his role. He might have intended to impose order on a shocking scene, but while he did not suffer himself, he had spent days surrounded by suffering. His nature was such

35   that his impulse had to be a bellow of 'Pull yourselves together!' But he was silent.

From 'A Love Child' by Doris Lessing in a book of short stories entitled
The Grandmothers (2003)

>> Task 3.3

1. Sum up in your own words what the writer means by 'The Bay of Biscay was doing its worst' (line 1). Your writing should be one paragraph long.

2. Explain what you learn from the passage about the history of this ship.

3. Summarise the specific problems of being on E Deck.

4. What does the vocabulary which Doris Lessing uses to describe Sergeant Perkins in the last paragraph tell you about his personality? Look closely at every word. Think about his appearance, actions and words. Comment in as much detail as you can.

>> Task 3.4

Choose two of the three passages (A, B and C) and work out how they are similar and how they are different. Remember that, although all three have things in common, each is a different genre. Passage A is 19th century travel writing. Passage B is an account of a scientific adventure and Passage C is historical fiction (written in the early 21st century looking back at the 1940s).

When you look for similarities consider:

- similar metaphors
- the effect of rough sea on passengers
- comedy
- sensuous writing – such as focus on sounds, smells and tastes.

Try discussing this in a pair or small group. Then you might work your thoughts into a joint or individual short essay in which you compare and contrast the two passages you have chosen.

Now read these three passages of poetry and do the tasks which follow.

> **Passage D (i)**
>
> Samuel Taylor Coleridge's best-known poem was first published in 1798 in a book of ground-breaking poems called The Lyrical Ballads. The volume consisted of poems by Coleridge and his friend William Wordsworth. One of the most powerful poems ever written in English, 'The Rime of the Ancient Mariner' is the tale of a mysterious old sailor telling a startled wedding guest the supernatural story of his voyage to Antarctica. The ship suffered terrible misfortune because - the mariner believes - he shot an albatross and brought bad luck on all his comrades. Coleridge had read the much earlier report by George Shelvocke (Passage D (ii)) which gave him the idea for the poem.

1   'And now the storm-blast came, and he
    Was tyrannous and strong:
    He struck with his o'ertaking wings,
    And chased us south along.

5   With sloping masts and dipping prow,
    As who pursued with yell and blow
    Still treads the shadow of his foe,
    And foward bends his head,
    The ship drove fast, loud roared the blast,
10 And southward aye we fled.

    And now there came both mist and snow,
    And it grew wondrous cold:
    And ice, mast-high, came floating by,
    As green as emerald.

15 And through the drifts the snowy clifts
    Did send a dismal sheen:
    Nor shapes of men nor beasts we ken—
    The ice was all between.

The ice was here, the ice was there,
20   The ice was all around:
It cracked and growled, and roared and howled,
Like noises in a swound!

At length did cross an Albatross,
Through the fog it came;
25   As it had been a Christian soul,
We hailed it in God's name.

It ate the food it ne'er had eat,
And round and round it flew.
The ice did split with a thunder-fit;
30   The helmsman steered us through!

And a good south wind sprung up behind;
The Albatross did follow,
And every day, for food or play,
Came to the mariner's hollo!

35   In mist or cloud, on mast or shroud,
It perched for vespers nine;
Whiles all the night, through fog-smoke white,
Glimmered the white moonshine.'

'God save thee, ancient Mariner,
40   From the fiends that plague thee thus!—
Why look'st thou so?'—'With my crossbow
I shot the Albatross.'

From 'The Rime of the Ancient Mariner' by Samuel Taylor Coleridge (1798)

*Illustration by David Jones from
the Rime of the Ancient Mariner*

Passage D (ii)

1   At seven in the evening, as they were furling the main-sail, one William Camell cry'd
    out, that his hands and fingers were so benumb'd that he could not hold himself, but
    before those that were next to him could come to his assistance, he fell down and
    was drown'd.

5   The cold is certainly much more insupportable in these, than in the same Latitudes to
    the Northward, for, although we were pretty much advanced in the summer season,
    and had the days very long. Yet we had continual squals [sic] of sleet, snow and rain,
    and the heavens were perpetually hid from us by gloomy dismal clouds. In short one
    would think it impossible that any thing living could subsist in so rigid a climate; and
10 indeed, we all observed, that we had not had the sight of one fish of any kind, since
    we were come to the Southward of the streights [sic] of le Mair, nor one sea-bird,
    except a disconsolate black Albatross, who accompanied us for several days, hovering
    about us as if he had lost himself, till Hatley, (my second Captain) observing, in one
    of his melancholy fits, that this bird was always hovering near us, imagin'd, from his
15 colour, that it might be some ill omen. That which, I suppose, induced him the more
    to encourage his superstition, was the continued series of contrary tempestuous
    winds, which had oppress'd us ever since we had got into this sea. But be that as it
    would, he, after some fruitless attempts, at length, shot the Albatross, not doubting
    (perhaps) that we should have a fair wind after it.

    A report, 'Albatross Shot', by George Shelvocke, 1st October 1719

>> Task 3.5

1. Explain why the sailors in Passage D (i) were so pleased to see the albatross.

2. Choose three words or short phrases from Passage D (i) which strike you as
    particularly powerful. Explain why you chose them. You might, for example,
    mention the way the poet uses words for their sounds.

3. Why does Hatley shoot the bird in Passage D (ii)? Do you think Coleridge's mariner is
    reasoning in the same way?

4. Look at Coleridge's rhymes. Explain how they drive the poem forward. Answer in as
    much detail as you can.

Passage E

Alan Ross served in the Royal Navy during World War Two and, ten years later, published a volume of poetry based on some of his experiences. In this dramatic poem he gives us a ship sunk by enemy action and explores the way it affected the men who survived. His understated style is very moving.

Survivors

1 With the ship burning in their eyes
The white faces float like refuse
In the darkness—the water screwing
Oily circles where the hot steel lies.

5 They clutch with fingers frozen into claws
The lifebelts thrown from a destroyer,
And see, between the future's doors.
The gasping entrance of the sea.

Taken on board as many as lived, who
10 Had a mind left for living and the ocean,
They open eyes running with surf,
Heavy with the grey ghosts of explosion.

The meaning is not yet clear,
When daybreak died in the smile—
15 And the mouth remained stiff
And grinning, stupid for a little while.

But soon they joke, easy and warm,
As men will who have died once
Yet somehow were able to find their way—
20 Muttering this was not included in their pay.

Later, sleepless at night, the brain spinning
With cracked images, they won't forget
The confusion and the oily dead,
Nor yet the casual knack of living.

'Survivors' by Alan Ross, 1955

Task 3.6

1. Summarise in your own words the story behind this poem. You could begin:
   A warship has just sunk and its crew are in the water. Some men …

2. What do think the poet means by (a) a mind left for living (line 10) and (b) the oily dead? (line 23)

3. Write as fully as you can about the phrases (a) fingers frozen into claws (b) stupid for a little while (c) cracked images.

Passage F

The Duke of Clarence is a prisoner in the Tower of London on the orders of his brother, the villainous Richard III (1452-1485) as presented by William Shakespeare in his famous play based on the king's reign. Most modern historians believe that Richard actually ruled quite well, but many people, perhaps including Shakespeare, were keen to discredit him for political reasons in the 16th century. In this passage Clarence, deeply disturbed and frightened - for good reason as it turns out - is describing his nightmares to a friendly guard.

1	O Lord! methought what pain it was to drown:
	Methoughts I saw a thousand fearful wrecks;
	Ten thousand men that fishes gnaw'd upon;
	Wedges of gold, great anchors, heaps of pearl,
5	Inestimable stones, unvalu'd jewels,
	All scattered in the bottom of the sea:
	Some lie in dead men's skulls, and in those holes
	Where eyes did once inhabit, there were crept—
	As 'twere in scorn of eyes—reflecting gems,
10	Which woo'd the slimy bottom of the deep,
	And mock'd the dead bones that lay scatter'd by.

From *Richard III*, Act 1, scene 4 by William Shakespeare (1591)

>> Task 3.7

Compare Passage F with one or more of the other prose or poetry passages in this chapter. Look at Shakespeare's language and the way he conveys Clarence's fear. How does it compare, for example, with the fear of the men in Passage E, Passages D(i) and D(ii) or Passage C? Discuss your ideas with a partner. Then take turns to explain your views to another pair in the class.

Writing about literature

When you are comparing two pieces of text link your argument with words phrases and sentences such as:

However …
Poet X, unlike Poet Y, suggests …
Like Poet B, Poet C evokes …
On the other hand …
Author K does this too. For example …
Poet F's point of view is different/similar
In contrast …
Similarly …

Study this short example which compares and contrasts some aspects of Alan Ross's poem:

> And see, between the future's doors.
> The gasping entrance of the sea.

with Shakespeare's:

> What dreadful noise of waters in mine ears;
> What ugly sights of death within mine eyes!

Both poets are describing fear of drowning at sea and both graphically evoke the terror of glimpsing the greedy 'gasping' sea and the 'ugly sights of death'. Ross, however – his words were written over 350 years after Shakespeare's when conventions were different – writes more conversationally and without any obvious contriving. Shakespeare's two lines are carefully patterned so that the second echoes the first. Both start with 'What' and both end with 'mine ears/eyes'. Words like 'dreadful'/'ugly', 'noise'/'sights' and 'death'/'waters' are paired too. The relentless rhythm of this structure reinforces the sense of horror. On the other hand Ross's chilling personification of the sea as something monstrous gasping to swallow prey and the image of the men in the water glimpsing their probable fate 'between the future's doors' is, like Shakespeare's two lines, also very sinister.

Personal Writing

>> Task 3.8

1. Write a personal account, in the form of a letter, of an occasion when you have been at sea. Decide whether you are going to aim for a light-hearted, comic tone like Dickens or Heyerdahl or whether you want to be more serious. Make up your mind before you start, to whom your letter is addressed.

2. Imagine you are a news journalist interviewing, after the voyage, one of the men aboard the ship described in 'A Love Child' or one of Alan Ross's survivors. Write your article for a newspaper, a magazine or for a news website such as http://news.bbc.co.uk.

3. Write a poem about the sea and/or travelling on it.

4. Read one of the books recommended in the 'Wide Range Reading' section of this chapter and write a review of it for the school magazine.

5. Imagine a meeting between the Duke of Clarence in *Richard III*, the character of the wedding guest addressed in Coleridge's poem and a group of Alan Ross's survivors. How would the conversation go? Write it either as dialogue – as if it were part of a story – or set it out like a play.

6. Write about the sea in any way you wish.

Writing tip

When you write a book review use Post-it notes (or similar) to make notes as you go. Stick these inside the cover of the book as you fill them up. Write on the Post-its the page and line numbers of anything you might want to quote or which seems particularly interesting. When you 'read to review' keep part of your mind on what you will write when you have finished the book. When you have finished reading you can detach the Post-its and stick them side by side on your desk or table – and there is your material. All you have to do is to work out how to organise it. Aim to write very specifically and in detail about a few aspects of the book rather than trying to skate over all of it. Vague statements such as 'This is a great book and I recommend it highly' do not help because they could be applied to any book.

WORD BANK

The word **maritime**, which Thor Heyerdahl uses, comes from the Latin word *mare* – sea. We also get a number of English words from the Latin words *aqua* – water and *navis* – a ship. Use the words in Task 3.9 derived from these three roots, in sentences of your own.

>> Task 3.9

1.	aquatic	6.	naval
2.	marine	7.	aqueduct
3.	navigable	8.	marigram
4.	aquasports	9.	aquarist
5.	navicular	10.	aquamarine

Doris Lessing uses the word **claustrophobia**. It means **an unnatural fear of enclosed spaces**. The word was coined in the 19th century from the Greek word *phobos* – fear and the Latin word *claustrum* – an enclosed space such as a cell.

>> Task 3.10

Write definitions for these phobias. Each is an unnatural fear of something:

1. aquaphobia
2. arachnophobia
3. xenophobia
4. agoraphobia
5. technophobia

Note: a person who suffers from a phobia is known as a -phobe. So someone with a fear of heights is an **acrophobe**. Someone who hates anything new is a **neophobe** and so on.

>> Task 3.11

Work with a partner. Choose a paragraph (or part of one) each from Passage A, Passage B or Passage C. Spend a few minutes studying it, looking particularly at the spelling of unfamiliar words. Then take it in turns to dictate the other's chosen paragraph. When you have both finished check your written work carefully with the original printed in this book and revise the spellings of any words you got wrong.

Look carefully at these sentences:

(a) Next day we were visited by tunnies, bonitos, and dolphins.

(b) The unprovoked attack was quickly forgiven by the injured party.

(c) The deck was crowded with men.

Each of these is expressed in the **passive voice**.

Had they been expressed in the alternative – **active voice** – they might have read like this:

(d) Tunnies, bonitos and dolphins visited us the next day.

(e) The injured party quickly forgave the unprovoked attack.

(f) Men crowded the deck.

Look carefully at the differences:

- When the verb in sentence (a) is in the passive voice its subject is 'we'. When it is in the active voice its subject is 'Tunnies, bonitos and dolphins'. Note also that when the verb is in the passive voice it does not govern a direct object.

- Some of the verb forms have changed. In sentence (a) 'were visited' becomes 'visited' and in sentence (b) 'was quickly forgiven' becomes 'forgave'.

- Sentences in the passive voice need an extra preposition to make it clear who or what is performing the action – usually 'by' but can occasionally be something else such as 'with'.

- A sentence in the passive voice is usually longer.

So which should you use?

Most people argue that the active voice is simpler and more direct and therefore usually better. That is why a computer grammar checker will often point out that you are using the passive voice and ask you if you want to change it.

On the other hand the passive voice is more formal and useful in, for instance, scientific writing.

It is also a matter of emphasis. The first item (noun or noun phrase) in a sentence tends to be the one the reader (or listener) is most aware of. Did Doris Lessing in sentence (c) want to stress the men or the deck?

In practice good writers use a mixture in order to vary the shapes of their sentence, but generally the active is more usual, especially in fiction.

Use of the passive voice can also be sloppy and ambiguous. This catch-line appeared over a news article in *The Daily Telegraph* on 11th January 2008:

> Horses left starving in field saved by RSPCA

Did the RSPCA save the horses or the field?

> RSPCA saves horses left starving in field

… would have been much better.

>> Task 3.12

Strengthen your understanding of how the active and passive voices work by changing these sentences from one to the other. The first five are in the passive voice and should be changed to active. Numbers (6) to (10) are in the active voice. Rewrite them as passive. Change the word order, verb forms and so on as much as you need to:

1. The dog was seen by the cat.
2. The meal was enjoyed by everyone.
3. It was reported by *The Times* that crime figures had risen.
4. The streets were filled with crowds.
5. In the Beethoven piece the accompaniment was played by Jessica Jones.
6. Most people like visiting the cinema.
7. Thor Heyerdahl built a raft in 1946.
8. Doris Lessing won the Nobel Prize for Literature.
9. Some say that money is the root of all evil.
10. Coleridge and Wordsworth published *Lyrical Ballads* at the end of the 18th century.

Only and other adverbs

Look at these sentences:

(a) We only ate salad that evening.

(b) Only we ate salad that evening.

(c) We ate only salad that evening.

(d) We ate salad only that evening.

The only difference is the position of 'only' but each sentence means something different:

(a) We only ate salad that evening. (We didn't, for example, grow it or wash it)

(b) Only we ate salad that evening. (Others chose something else)

(c) We ate only salad that evening. (We ate nothing but salad)

(d) We ate salad only that evening. (We had eaten salad very recently)

Think very carefully about what you mean when you use the word 'only'. Adverbs such as 'just' and 'even' are often carelessly placed in newspapers and books too which makes their expression less precise than it should be.

Get into the habit of being aware of this. Take care in you own writing and watch out for errors in your reading – which you can then mentally correct!

>> Task 3.13

Reinforce your understanding of what sentences actually mean by writing explanations in brackets for the following as I have done above:

1. Marissa was just waiting.

2. Just Marissa was waiting.

3. Even George enjoyed the film.

4. George even enjoyed the film.

5. George enjoyed even the film.

6. Only my family booked the flight.

7. My family booked the flight only.

8. My family only booked the flight.

More speaking and listening activities

Prepare a talk for the class about disaster at sea – such as the sinking of the Titanic in 1912 or the loss of the passenger ferry Herald of Free Enterprise which capsized off the coast of Belgium in 1987.

Listen to a recording of Coleridge's 'The Rime of the Ancient Mariner'. Did you enjoy it? What did you like or dislike about it?

In a small group make up a story about a shipwreck. Rehearse how you will tell it – taking turns to speak. Then perform your story to another group.

In a small group read aloud and talk about the extract from 'The Rime of the Ancient Mariner' in this chapter and the factual report which inspired it. Which do you prefer and why? Do you like the poem any more or less because you know where Coleridge's idea came from?

The whole word in this 11-letter word wheel is used in one of the extracts which opens this chapter. Make as many words as you can from its letters, including the whole word. Each should be four letters or more. You must use the letter in the centre of the wheel in every word.

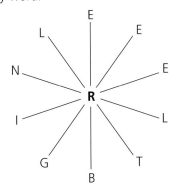

WIDE RANGE READING

All of these titles feature sea travel.

English Passengers by Matthew Kneale (2001) is a novel about a group of individuals who travel by ship to Tasmania (off Southern Australia) in the early 19th century – for a variety of reasons, some honourable and some not. The conditions on board ship are vividly described and events when they reach Tasmania are horrifying – not least because this is a novel based on historical fact.

Alone on a Wide Wide Sea by Michael Morpurgo (2006). Written for teenagers this lovely story is about the 21st century daughter of a man who was taken from Britain to Australia as a miserable orphan in the 1950s. She is determined to sail to the UK as her father always wanted to do. So she does it – alone. It's a gripping tale with a wonderful ending. The title is a quotation from 'The Rime of the Ancient Mariner'.

Taking on the World (2002) and **Race Against Time** (2005) by Ellen MacArthur. In 2001 Ellen MacArthur, aged 24, became the youngest person ever to sail single-handed around the world. She was also the fastest woman ever to have done it. These two exciting books tell the story of her voyage and her life.

Aku-aku: The Secret of Easter Island by Thor Heyerdahl (1958). Tucked away in the South Pacific, over 2,000 miles from the nearest land (Chile), Easter Island is very small and remote yet it has 887 huge, ancient carved stone statues. There are many theories about their history. This fascinating book is Heyerdahl's contribution to the debate.

One Summer's Grace by Libby Purves (1989). As well as being one of Britain's best-known journalists and a fine novelist, Libby Purves is a highly-experienced sailor who writes for yachting magazines. In the summer of 1988 she spent several months sailing all the way round the coast of Britain with her husband and two young children. This colourful and amusing book allows you to share their experiences.

The Cruel Sea by Nicholas Monsarrat (1951). This is a novel based on the author's experiences during the Second World War in ships dangerously crossing the Atlantic in convoy, often under attack from German submarines. There is a strong, satisfying love story at the heart of this highly recommended novel. A good (black and white) film, starring Jack Hawkins – now a classic – was made of it too.

Moby Dick by Herman Melville (1851). A very famous story about Captain Ahab's quest to catch and kill a white whale which had bitten off his leg. It's a very dramatic novel which is hard to put down once you get going.

Lord Jim by Joseph Conrad (1900). Jim is chief mate on a ship carrying pilgrims in Eastern waters in one of Conrad's best novels. Having faced an enquiry about his behaviour during an emergency at sea, Jim ends up running a trading station where he is deeply respected and becomes known as 'Lord' Jim – although that is not the end of the story.

MOVING ON

- Many composers have been inspired by the sea. Listen to the Hebrides Overture (Mendelssohn), Sea Interludes from Peter Grimes (Britten), La Mer (Debussy), Sea Symphony (Vaughan Williams) or Sea Pictures (Elgar), for example. Decide how well you think they evoke the sounds and atmosphere of the sea.

- Read the opening scene of Shakespeare's play *The Tempest* in which sailors are struggling for survival in a storm at sea.

- Find out about the life and work of Charles Dickens. Make a poster about him for the classroom wall or prepare a short presentation for the rest of the class.

- For fun and to add a few more, some of them deliciously obscure, –phobia words to your word bank have a look at www.changethatsrightnow.com and click on 'Complete list of Phobias'.

NB: 's' in website address is correct.

READY FOR A REAL CHALLENGE?

Write a story-telling poem using the rhyme scheme and rhythmic pattern that Coleridge does in 'The Rime of the Ancient Mariner'.

Find, and make a study of, Matthew Arnold's poem 'Dover Beach'. It's in many anthologies including *The New Dragon Book of Verse* or you can get it from a poetry site on the internet.

4 Let Slip the Dogs of War

What causes war? Human beings have always fought each other for territory and power – and that means wars. Brainstorm with a partner all the wars in history you can think of. Sadly you will almost certainly run out of time before you run out of wars. Many wars are being fought in different parts of the world today too.

Inevitably feelings, experiences and views about these wars have inspired writing in almost every genre: factual, eye-witness accounts (known as 'reportage'), poetry, novels, plays and so on as the five passages which open this chapter show.

The First World War (1914–1918), in particular, led to some outstanding literature, especially poetry. I have, however, deliberately avoided this in these five extracts because I think you will probably have read some of that before and I want to introduce you to something new. So, instead, we range across 27 centuries from the 7th century BC to the Korean War in the 1950s.

The title of this chapter is a quotation from Shakespeare's *Julius Caesar*, a play whose second half is dominated by a war.

Passage A

1 Most stories about Viking raids in Britain in the 'Dark Ages' (between the departure of the Romans and the arrival of the Normans) are written from the British point
5 of view. Pauline Chandler's lively adventure story for young readers tells the story of Beren - a 9th century Viking princess who narrates. She arrives in Britain with her
10 followers partly to overpower the Saxon residents. She also has a mission, however, to avenge her dead father by overcoming her wicked uncle - Vasser. It is quite an
15 original idea for the central character and narrator to be female in a novel about
20 fighting and war.

Vasser was strong-armed, battle-hard, but I was quick on my feet. Othinn would decide the outcome.

Time stalled as the bloodsurge came on me and bathed me in Othinn's fire. I knew there were warriors all around us, shouting, as Saxons streamed out of the monastery to join battle. I knew when Einar rode to the fight, leading men of the fyrd, to deal blows with hayfork and scythe. I saw fists raised and the flash and fall of blades, but it was none of my business. My eyes were fixed on Vassar's sword and I heard only the ding and dint of the iron as we traded blows, edge to edge.

The knock of his blade jarred my bones, then, with a knock of my own, I caught the top of his sword arm and a line of blood oozed from the wound. For reply Vasser drew his knife and now thrust at me with two blades. Like a young man he crouched

in front of me, making brief passes in front of me with his knives, to keep me off
centre. I crouched to echo his stance, but kept my blades, sword and knife, poised to
strike, stone still as a hawk's head as she looks at her prey.

'Thorkil was weak', Vasser said. Yet your mother preferred him. That Saxon trull. Like
a filthy vixen she waited on him ...'

I sprang at him. He caught me and pushed me back. I wrestled with him and he took
my sword from me and threw it away. He held me with one arm under my chin,
pressing back my head against his chest, as he let loose poisonous words.

'Fierce fighter, though. You have her fire. Even without weapons she almost did for
me.' With what strength I had left I thrust myself away from him. Panting, I watched
him as you would watch a venomous snake. 'Not strong enough, in the end.'

Vasser called his warriors to stop the fight. With deep drawn breaths, they did so,
and my force also lowered their weapons. They fell back to give us room. Vasser now
sheathed his sword and we stood facing each other, each holding a knife, to finish it.

'I killed her, Beren', he whispered. 'Thorkil suspected, but could not prove it. I did it. I
killed them both.'

Rage filled me with one thought. To stab and stab, and stab again, until Vasser's
flesh gaped with wounds. In a single move, I leapt for him and jabbed my knife up to
his jaw, but he jerked his head away and the blow missed its aim. Off balance, I
stumbled, and Vasser knocked the knife from my hand, put his fist in my hair and
dragged me upright, turning me round to show me to my warriors.

'Before I kill her, who will fight me for her life?' No one moved. Vasser kicked the
back of my thighs until I fell to my knees. 'No one, it seems. You are without a
friend.' He put the blade to my throat and jabbed lightly. It was not sharp, a mild
sting only, but it grew warmer with each breath.

'Now I have you where you should be', Vasser bent down to murmur in my ear.
'When you die, as you surely will – the venom on my blade is slow-acting but certain
– they will not blame me. All saw you challenge me. You brought this upon yourself.
Die, then Berengeria. Though I'm truly sorry for it. You have your mother's eyes.'

'I give her back to you!' he shouted. He let me go and I slumped forward, my face
pressing upon the cool ground. 'Wulf's queen has learned her lesson. There will be
no more talk of rebellion and no more talk of blood debts.'

Vasser was carefully wiping his knife. My fingers and feet were cold, but I couldn't
move to warm them, and a gradual darkness seeped in at the edge of my sight.

60

'Vasser Wulf!' someone shouted from the top of the monastery fence. I blinked to see who it was and my bleared eyes fixed on one face among all, the face of one who was about to claim a blood debt of his own.

From his vantage point atop the monastery fence, Cedd raised his bow, drew back his hand, then let loose a fatal dart. Above me Vasser stood for a single breath, then fell back like a toppled tree, the shaft of Cedd's dart sticking out of his neck. I gazed at Cedd and saw the face of my rescuer, the face of a friend.

From *Viking Girl* by Pauline Chandler (2007)

>> Task 4.1

1. Why is Beren beginning to faint (line 57 '... a gradual darkness seeped in at the edge of my sight')?

   _____

2. Summarise what you learn about Vasser from this passage. Consider what he does and what he says. Use your own words but incorporate short quotations (enclosed in inverted commas) from the passage.

   _____

3. Who is Othinn?

   _____

4. What do you think is meant by a 'blood debt'?

Passage B

1 Korea had been a Japanese colony since 1910. After the defeat of Japan in the Second World War (1939-1945) the country was split. The north was taken

5 over by Soviet Russia. The South was governed under the supervision of an American military regime. Border skirmishes led to all-out war in 1950 which

10 did not end until 1953 and which involved many thousands of US and British soldiers as well as Russians and Koreans.

15 North and South Korea remain separate – and very different - countries today. In this piece of reportage a female US journalist reports from the front line.

General Walker was very correct and absolutely frank with me.

He said he still felt that the front was no place for a woman, but that orders were orders and that from now on I could be assured of absolutely equal treatment.

'If something had happened to you, an American woman', the general explained, 'I would have gotten a terrible press. The American public might never have forgiven me. So please be careful and don't get yourself killed or captured.'

General Walker kept his promise of equal treatment, and from then on, so far as

20 the United States Army was concerned, I went about my job with no more hindrance than the men.

Despite large-scale reinforcements, our troops were still falling back fast. Our lines made a huge semicircle around the city of Taegu. The main pressure at that time was

25 from the northwest down the Taejon-Taegu road. But a new menace was developing with frightening rapidity way to the southwest. For the Reds, making a huge arc around our outnumbered troops, were sending spearheads to the south coast of Korea hundreds of miles to our rear. They hoped to strike along the coast at Pusan, the vital port through which most of our supplies funnelled.

30 It was at this time that General Walker issued his famous 'stand or die' order. The 1st Cavalry and 25th Division were freshly arrived. Like the 24th Division before them, the new outfits had to learn for themselves how to cope with this Indian-style warfare for which they were so unprepared. Their soldiers were not yet battle-toughened. Taking into account the overwhelming odds, some front-line generals

35 worried about the performance of their men and told us so privately.

General Walker put his worries on the record and at the same time issued his 'no-retreat' order. In a visit to the 25th Division front at Sangju in the north, he told assembled headquarters and field officers, 'I am tired of hearing about lines being

straightened. There will be no more
retreating. Reinforcements are coming,
but our soldiers have to be impressed
that they must stand or die. If they fall
back they will be responsible for the
lives of hundreds of Americans. A
Dunkerque in Korea would be a
terrible blow from which it would be
hard to recover.'

Immediately General Walker, in a
massive straightening operation of his
own, took the entire 25th Division out
of the line there north of Taegu. He
sent them barrelling to the southwest
front to bear the brunt of the enemy's
attempt to break through to Pusan.

*South Koreans fleeing from the battle zone
and American soldiers marching to the Front
as reinforcements, August 1950*

The operation was skilfully done and the reshuffled troops arrived just in time.

To fill the gap vacated by the 25th Division, the 1st Cavalry and the South Koreans
were pulled back in a tightening operation in which we relinquished about fifty
miles, but we attained a smaller, better-integrated defense arc.

It is certainly a tribute to General Walker that in the period when he had so few
troops on hand and no reserves at all he was able to juggle his forces geographically
so as to hold that great semicircle from the coast down the Naktong River valley to
Masan on the southern coast.

I reached the southwest front in time for the 25th's first big battle after the 'stand or
die' order. By luck I happened to be the only daily newspaperman on the scene. The
rest of the correspondents were at Pusan covering the debarkation of the United
States Marines. My colleague on the Herald Tribune had selected the marine landing
for his own. So I left Pusan and hitchhiked my way west.

At Masan I borrowed a jeep from the 724th Ordnance and drove in the dusk over the
beautiful mountains that wind west and overlook the deep blue waters of Masan
Bay. The jewel-bright rice paddies in the long, steep-sided valley held a soft sheen
and the war seemed far away. But only a few nights later the sharp blue and orange
tracer bullets were flicking across the valley's mouth until dawn.

*From War in Korea: The Report of a Woman Combat Correspondent
by Marguerite Higgins (1951)*

>> Task 4.2

1. What impression do you get of General Walker from this passage? Look at what he says and does. Answer as fully as you can in your own words but incorporate short quotations from the passage, enclosed in inverted commas.

2. What does the writer mean by 'A Dunkerque in Korea' (line 45)? (Dunkerque is a port in Northern France often spelled 'Dunkirk' in English.)

3. In what ways is the account of (the real) Marguerite Higgins similar to, or different from, the (fictional) writing of Beren in Passage A? You might like to consider:

   • their both being women

   • their respective roles in the fighting

   • the style of story telling

   • the difference between fiction and reportage.

Passage C

1

Britain was at war with France in Europe for almost 25 years (with a 14-month respite in 1802/3). Known as the

5 Revolutionary Wars before 1802 and the Napoleonic Wars after 1803, the conflict finally ended in a one-day battle at Waterloo in Belgium in 1815. The British

10 were led to victory by the Duke of Wellington against Napoleon Bonaparte and the French. Like the reportage from the Korean War above this is an eye-

15 witness account by a British officer of some of the events of the afternoon.

At the commencement of the Action a Corps of Belgians of from 8,000 to 10,000 men were formed in line in front of the 5th Division, but soon after they were attacked and their skirmishers driven in on their line, the whole of them retired through the 5th Division, and were no more seen during the Action. After this the Enemy made several severe attacks on the 5th Division. About two or three o'clock in the afternoon a Column between 3,000 to 4,000 men advanced to the hedge at the roadside which leads from the main road near La Haye Sainte beyond the left

20 of our position. Previous to this the 92nd had been lying down under cover of the position when they were immediately ordered to stand to their arms, Major-General Sir Denis Pack calling out at the same time, '92nd everything has given way on your

25

right and left and you must charge this Column', upon which he ordered four deep to be formed and closed into the centre. The Regiment, which was then within about 20 yards of the Column, fired a volley into them. The Enemy on reaching the hedge at the side of the road had ordered arms, and were in the act of shouldering them when they received the volley from the 92nd.

30

35

The Scots Greys came up at this moment, and doubling round our flanks and through our centre where openings were made for them, both Regiments charged together, calling out 'Scotland for ever', and the Scots Greys actually walked over this Column, and in less than three minutes it was totally destroyed, 2,000, besides killed and wounded, of them having been made prisoners, and two of their Eagles captured. The grass field in which the Enemy was formed, which only an instant before as green and smooth as the 15 acres in Phoenix Park, was in a few minutes covered with killed and wounded, knapsacks and their contents, arms, accoutrements, etc., literally strewed all over, that to avoid stepping on either one or the other was quite impossible; in fact one could hardly believe, had he not witnessed it, that such complete destruction could have been effected in so short a time.

40

Some of the French soldiers who were lying wounded were calling out *'Vive L'Empereur'*, and others firing their muskets at our men who had advanced past them in pursuit of the flying Enemy.

Report by Lieutenant R Winchester, 92nd Highlanders of the Charge of the Scots Greys and 92nd Highlanders, 2–3 p.m, Waterloo, 18th June 1815.

>> Task 4.3

1. Explain in your own words how the large group of nearly 10,000 Belgians was beaten.

2. Compare Passage C with Passage B. Look closely at the detail and answer as fully as you can. Use these points as a guideline:

   - level of accurate reporting

   - vocabulary

   - how a professional journalist's style differs from that of a soldier writing a report

   - differences between British English of 1815 and American English of 1953

   - anything else which strikes you as interesting.

Passage D

Shakespeare's Henry V tells his version of the story of England's king who led an invasion of France in the 15th century. The English - tired, sick and demoralised - are about to face the French in a decisive battle at Agincourt in 1415. The French have a much larger army. They are fresh and they are on home ground. The Duke of Westmoreland mutters that he wishes that the English had more men which triggers the splendid, moving speech below from the king. Henry wants to motivate his men. It works. The next day they beat the French - against all the odds.

1
What's he that wishes so?
My cousin Westmoreland? No, my fair cousin:
If we are mark'd to die, we are enow
To do our country loss; and if to live,
5
The fewer men, the greater share of honour.
God's will! I pray thee, wish not one man more.
By Jove, I am not covetous for gold,
Nor care I who doth feed upon my cost;
It yearns me not if men my garments wear;
10
Such outward things dwell not in my desires:
But if it be a sin to covet honour,
I am the most offending soul alive.
No, faith, my coz, wish not a man from England:
God's peace! I would not lose so great an honour
15
As one man more, methinks, would share from me
For the best hope I have. O, do not wish one more!
Rather proclaim it, Westmoreland, through my host,
That he which hath no stomach to this fight,
Let him depart; his passport shall be made
20
And crowns for convoy put into his purse:
We would not die in that man's company
That fears his fellowship to die with us.
This day is called the feast of Crispian:
He that outlives this day, and comes safe home,
25
Will stand a tip-toe when the day is named,
And rouse him at the name of Crispian.
He that shall live this day, and see old age,
Will yearly on the vigil feast his neighbours,
And say 'To-morrow is Saint Crispian:'

30 Then will he strip his sleeve and show his scars.
And say 'These wounds I had on Crispin's day.'
Old men forget: yet all shall be forgot,
But he'll remember with advantages
What feats he did that day: then shall our names.
35 Familiar in his mouth as household words
Harry the king, Bedford and Exeter,
Warwick and Talbot, Salisbury and Gloucester,
Be in their flowing cups freshly remember'd.
This story shall the good man teach his son;
40 And Crispin Crispian shall ne'er go by,
From this day to the ending of the world,
But we in it shall be remember'd;
We few, we happy few, we band of brothers;
For he to-day that sheds his blood with me
45 Shall be my brother; be he ne'er so vile,
This day shall gentle his condition:
And gentlemen in England now a-bed
Shall think themselves accursed they were not here,
And hold their manhoods cheap whiles any speaks
50 That fought with us upon Saint Crispin's day.

From *Henry V* by William Shakespeare (1599)

*Kenneth Branagh in the 1989
film version of* Henry V

Passage E

Hezekiah was the King of Judah in the 7th century BC. According to the Bible story (2 Kings, Ch 18, v 13), Judah was attacked by the Assyrians whose king was Sennacherib. Because the war was going badly for him Hezekiah prayed very hard. God sent 'the angel of the Lord' to the Assyrian camp in the night to kill most of the men there, although not Sennacherib himself. The Assyrian king escaped only to be killed later by his own sons. Here Byron's colourful, rhythmic poem imagines the scene in the Assyrian camp.

The Destruction of Sennacherib

1
The Assyrian came down like the wolf on the fold,
And his cohorts were gleaming in purple and gold;
And the sheen of their spears was like stars on the sea,
When the blue wave rolls nightly on deep Galilee.

5
Like the leaves of the forest when Summer is green,
That host with their banners at sunset were seen:
Like the leaves of the forest when Autumn hath blown,
That host on the morrow lay withered and strown.

For the Angel of Death spread his wings on the blast,
10
And breathed in the face of the foe as he pass'd,
And the eyes of the sleepers wax'd deadly and chill,
And their hearts but once heaved, and for ever grew still!

And there lay the steed with his nostril all wide,
But through it there roll'd not the breath of his pride;
15
And the foam of his gasping lay white on the turf,
And cold as the spray of the rock-beating surf.

And there lay the rider distorted and pale,
With the dew on his brow, and the rust on his mail:
And the tents were all silent, the banners alone,
20
The lances unlifted, the trumpets unblown.

And the widows of Ashur are loud in their wail,
And the idols are broke in the temple of Baal;
And the might of the Gentile, unsmote by the sword,
Hath melted like snow in the glance of the Lord!

'The Destruction of Sennacherib' by Lord Byron (1815)

>> Task 4.4

1. In Passage D what does Henry offer any man who doesn't want to fight?

2. Why, according to Henry, should his men be proud to be involved? Summarise his argument in your own words. Write two or three sentences.

3. How does Byron make the Assyrians seem glamorous and strong? Quote from the poem in your answer.

4. Choose and write in as much detail as you can about three phrases or lines from Passage E which you particularly like or find interesting.

5. List all the differences you can think of between Passages D and E. Are there any similarities? Discuss this with a partner or in a group before you write.

6. Although Passage D is an extract from a play it is also a piece of poetry. Which appeals to you most – Passage D or Passage E? Use short quotations from the poems – putting them in inverted commas within your sentences – to explain your reasons.

Writing about literature

Sometimes prose writing – particularly fiction – gets its effects from borrowing techniques from poetry. This is always worth commenting on in depth if you spot it.

Consider the example below of how you might write about this sentence from Passage A:

> I crouched to echo his stance, but kept my blades, sword and knife, poised to strike, stone still as a hawk's head as she looks at her prey.

Chandler's sibilant vocabulary in the repeated 's' sounds ('stance', 'sword', 'poised', 'strike', 'stone', 'still', 'she' – and others) at the beginnings of words and within them gives this sentence a very appropriate sense of hissing menace as Beren faces her opponent in this fight to the death. In places ('stone' 'still' 'stance') where the alliterative 's' is linked to a plosive 't' the effect is even more marked. You can almost hear and feel Beren's fear, aggression and determination. The hawk's head simile works well too. A hawk is a ruthless predator as Beren wants to be. It is also an apt image because although this novel was written in 2007, when pollution and urbanisation means that we see fewer birds of prey, a 9th century princess would probably have been very familiar with hawks and their behaviour – not least because of their use in sport.

➤➤ Task 4.5

Choose a sentence which interests you from any of the passages in this chapter and comment on it in detail.

Personal Writing

➤➤ Task 4.6

1. Imagine you are Vasser from Passage A. Write your account of the fight with Beren as if you were creating a section of a novel for young people.

2. Write a blog – a piece of reportage – about any event you have witnessed. Of course it need not be a fight or a war! It could be an accident, a visit to your school or area by a celebrity, a flood, something unexpected such as seeing three men carrying a grand piano along a street – or anything else you happen to have seen.

3. Take any dramatic *Bible* story (David and Goliath? Noah's Flood? Moses being found in the bulrushes? Daniel in the lion's den?) – there are plenty to choose from. Reread it and imagine how it would really have felt to be there. Write a poem in which you approach the event from an unusual angle.

4. Imagine you are trying to assemble a school team for a sports event. You are having trouble because your peers are, for some reason, reluctant. Write your own version of Henry V's famous 'St Crispin's Day' speech to inspire them. Use prose or verse.

5. Work out your views about war by discussing them with someone else or in a group. Then write your opinions in the form of an essay.

6. Write about war in any way you wish.

Writing tip

When you write a discursive essay such as the one suggested in 5 above, plan it very carefully in two stages.

There will usually be two sides to the argument: reasons for and against – or pros and cons. Use a blank sheet of A4 paper and make two columns. Jot down in note form all the arguments in favour of war (in this case) you can think of and all the reasons against it in the other column. Then add to your notes anyone whose views you want to quote and any examples you want to bring in.

That gives you the content of your essay in random form. Now organise it. Take another sheet of paper and work out how you will arrange the material in about five or six sections – each probably consisting of more than one paragraph and preceded by an introduction and followed by a conclusion.

It is often a good idea to state in your introduction something like 'There are five reasons I cannot be totally opposed to all war.' Then start your next paragraph. 'First …' When you are ready, write: 'My second point is …' Then, later, 'The third reason …' This way your structure is clear and your writing carefully thought out and logical without being repetitive.

WORD BANK

Henry V talks of men 'which hath no **stomach** for this fight'.

In modern English the word **stomach** – as a noun – usually means the muscular bag in the body where food is held until it has been partially digested. We also use it as a verb meaning **to bear**, **withstand** or **tolerate** – I cannot stomach bullying. Used literally it means unable to digest, for example, 'She cannot stomach shellfish'.

The word came into English in the 14th century via Old French from the Latin word *stomachus*. It had developed from the Greek word *stoma* which means a mouth. The Greeks and the Romans thought that all our emotions come from the stomach. So it is often used in literature of the past to suggest **appetites** other than hunger – sexual desire, for example.

In Shakespeare's time and after a **stomacher** was a **garment worn over the chest and stomach**. **Stomatology** (think of the Greek root) is the branch of medicine or dentistry concerned with diseases of the mouth.

A **vigil**, such as the one Henry V's men are facing, is **a purposeful, wakeful watch during the night** – often for religious reasons. It comes from the Latin verb *vigilo* to watch or be awake. The words **vigilance**, **vigilant** and **vigilante** – look them up if you don't know them – are all, of course, related. So is **invigilation**, which is what teachers do while students take exams.

Sheen is a lovely and interesting word – used by Byron and, nearly 150 years later, by Margerite Higgins. It means **a gleaming or glistening brightness** and comes from the Old English word *sciene*.

>> Task 4.7

Use these words – all taken from the passages in this chapter – in sentences of your own to show that you understand their meaning. Change the form of the word – from a verb to a noun, for example – if you wish:

1. relinquished
2. covetous
3. accoutrements
4. distorted
5. brunt
6. rapidity
7. accursed
8. fellowship
9. volley
10. skirmishers

>> Task 4.8

Work on these spellings with a partner. Test and coach each other until you each have them perfect:

1. poisonous
2. hindrance
3. skilful
4. column
5. immediately
6. reinforcements
7. Gloucester
8. Warwick
9. knapsack
10. previous
11. correspondent
12. geographically

NUTS AND BOLTS

Take great care with the use of 'both … and', 'either … or', and 'neither … nor'. Many people use them carelessly which can lead to confusion. They are another good example of word order which can affect meaning in English. Look at these sentences, each of which means something different:

Shakespeare and Byron both wrote fine poetry which communicates and inspires.
Shakespeare and Byron wrote fine poetry which both communicates and inspires.

Neither Shakespeare nor Byron wrote prose or expressed views about current events.
Shakespeare and Byron neither wrote prose nor expressed views about current events.

Talk about these sentences with a partner and work out what they each mean.

>> Task 4.9

Make up a 'base' sentence using 'both … and'. Then write as many variations on it as you can. Alter the word order and the punctuation if you need to.

Invent a 'base' sentence using 'neither … nor'. Then write as many variations on it as you can. Alter the word order and the punctuation as necessary.

Construct a 'base' sentence using 'either … or'. Then write as many variations on it as you can. Alter the word order and the punctuation if your sentences require it.

Apostrophe errors are some of the commonest mistakes in English. Learn to get it right.

You will have learned this before but here it is again if you need it:

REMEMBER an 's' at the end of a word usually shows that it is a plural noun (three wars, four soldiers, two guns, etc) or that it is part of a verb (Shakespeare writes, he walks, Jake laughs).

None of these needs an apostrophe.

No apostrophe, for instance, is needed anywhere in a sentence like this:

> Most of the girls in classes one, two and three enjoy hockey lessons, but Mavis Jeffreys insists that she prefers board games.

Eight words in this example end in 's'. None needs an apostrophe.

The apostrophe has two uses. It shows:

1. Possession.
2. That letters have been missed out.

1. To mark possession, the apostrophe comes immediately after the possessor noun and is followed by 's'. When the possessor is singular the apostrophe thus goes before the letter 's':

> Beren's sword is the sword possessed by Beren. (One girl – singular)

> A year's work is the work connected with, or possessed by, the year. (One term – singular)

When the possessor noun is plural the apostrophe still comes immediately after the possessor noun. Because this plural noun generally ends in 's', the apostrophe now comes after the letter 's':

> The Saxons' fort is the fort possessed by the Saxons. (More than one Saxon – plural)

> Three months' effort is an effort lasting, or possessed by, three months. (More than one month – plural)

Take care with words which already end in 's' or 'ss' in their singular or plural form. Exactly the same rules apply:

> The princess's dress (singular)
> Three actresses' autographs (plural)

St James's church (singular)
Mr Watts's class (singular)

Note that plural nouns which do not end in 's' – such as children and women – behave as if they were singular and take an apostrophe before the 's' when they are possessive. For example: Working men's club, children's games.

2. The apostrophe also stands in place of missing letters in contracted words such as:

wouldn't (would not)
o'clock (of the clock)
shan't (shall not)
C'bury (Canterbury – on road signs)
it's (it is or it has)

Be particularly careful with 'its' which means 'of it' and 'it's' which means 'it is' or 'it has'.

Learn this example:

It's a pity that our house has its windows so close to the next building.

Remember that far more words do NOT need an apostrophe than need one. Do not scatter apostrophes like confetti every time you see an 's'!

›› Task 4.10

Write these sentences with correct apostrophes:

1. Lord Byrons poem 'The Destruction of Sennacherib' has its origins in The Bible.

2. Prince Charles and the Duchess of Cornwall opened the towns new shopping centre.

3. Its been a while since we met the twins mother.

4. Weve invited several actresses to our schools open day.

5. King Charless reign ended abruptly in 1649.

6. Havent you asked Thomass sisters to the party?

4 Let Slip the Dogs of War

glish Year 9

More speaking and listening activities

Watch a film of
Henry V. Listen very carefully
to the words which are spoken.
Jot down as many memorable
phrases and lines as you can
remember afterwards. Some of
Shakespeare's most rousing
poetry is in this play.

Work in a pair. Take it in
turns to tell your partner about
a book you have read recently but
which he or she has not. Then join with
another pair. Take it in turns to tell the
other two about your partner's book.
Treat this as a listening activity and
do not take or use notes.

Organise a class
discussion or debate about war –
war in general or a specific current one.
You will need to read carefully in
preparation for this. Use the internet
(http://news.bbc.co.uk is a useful site) and
newspapers or websites connected with them.
Gather as much information as you can from as
many sources as possible. This will inform
your arguments and help you to present
well thought out views.

Hold a class 'War
Poetry Festival'. Each member
of the class finds a war poem he or
she likes or is moved by and prepares a
reading of it. Then on an agreed day you
all present your poems. If you have a
'signing up' system for people to state
in advance which poems they have
chosen you can avoid
duplication.

Book quiz

Try this book quiz. The answer to each clue is a book title or author. For example:

Clue: PP by JMB

Answer: *Peter Pan* by JM Barrie

Clue: TCT by GC

Answer: 'The Canterbury Tales' by Geoffrey Chaucer

1. GNMT by MM
2. NN by CD
3. AIW by LC
4. HPATPS by JKR
5. BB by AS

6. AMND by WS
7. TWITW by KG
8. TSK by PP
9. PAP by JA
10. TOTD by TH

11. KK by MM
12. THAPC by AAM
13. TWIW by WC
14. TSS by IS
15. M by WS

16. JE by CB
17. TRC by EEN
18. AF by GO
19. TLTWATW by CSL
20. S by DA

WIDE RANGE READING

Try these books which all feature war experiences.

The Trumpet Major by Thomas Hardy (1880) is set during the Napoleonic Wars when most people in Britain were, with good reason, deeply fearful that an invasion by the French was about to happen. Two men – one of whom is a trumpet-major with soldiers billeted nearby – are in love with the same girl who also has a third suitor. Inevitably this novel does not end happily for all characters! Although Hardy is writing 70 years after the period he is describing, he makes a very convincing job of the anxious atmosphere.

Gone with the Wind by Margaret Mitchell (1936) is set in Georgia during the American Civil war in the mid-19th century. Regarded by many as one of the greatest love stories ever told (perhaps after *Romeo and Juliet* and *Antony and Cleopatra*) the tale of Scarlett O'Hara, her three marriages and her many war-related separations from the wildly attractive, but risky, Rhett Butler makes a powerful read. There is a very famous film (1939) and more recently, a stage musical, based on this novel too.

Atonement by Ian McEwan (2002) tells the story of a couple who are forcibly separated in the 1930s when something goes wrong. Then he goes to war. The account of the retreat to Dunkirk across Northern France and the agony as the exhausted and frightened men wait to be rescued from the beaches is beautifully done and very graphic – unforgettable. The story is narrated by the girl's younger sister whose fault it is that the lovers are parted. Her life-long guilt lies behind the title. This novel was made into a fine film (2007) directed by Joe Wright starring Keira Knightley and James McAvoy. Read the book first and then decide what you think of the film.

Winter in Madrid by CF Sansom (2006) is set mostly in Spain during the Spanish Civil War (1936–1939) when many men from other countries such as Britain went to support Spanish objectors against General Franco and fascism – a 'battle for Spain' which Franco won. The terrible suffering of the Englishman at the centre of the story who is sent to a prison camp is gruelling. It's an exciting page-turner too, full of unexpected twists as characters turn out not to be quite what they seem.

Apache by Tanya Landman (2007) is aimed at teenagers. This is an unusual story about a girl who becomes a warrior in her American Indian tribe in the 19th century. At first it's fighting the Mexicans. Then come the land-hungry white settlers from the east. And at the same time Siki, the narrator, is dealing with growing up and feelings she doesn't quite understand for the older man who trains her to fight – and it's a tough training school. All in all it's a fine novel with a carefully researched background that most of us know little about. The characters are well done too.

The Way of the Warrior by Andrew Matthews (2007) is aimed at children a little younger than Year 9, so it's quite a quick and easy read. I mention it here because of its unusual background. It is set among the warring clans of 16th century Japan. Orphaned Jimmu trains to be a Samurai – a lethal fighter – because he has been led to believe that his destiny is to avenge his father. In fact, everything is not quite as it seems in this fast-paced story of loyalty, betrayal and deception.

War Horse (1982) and ***Private Peaceful*** (2003) are both short novels (really 'novellas') for younger readers by Michael Morpurgo. Both are set in the First World War. The first is the story of the horrors of the war from the point of view of a horse used in battle. The second is about a man who has been found guilty of cowardice – but was what he did really cowardly? – and is therefore due to be executed. Both are breathtakingly moving whatever your age.

Many poets have written movingly and well about war. Look in anthologies for the work of:

Wilfred Owen, Charles Causley, Siegfried Sassoon, John Dryden, Alan Ross, Rupert Brooke and many others.

MOVING ON

- Listen to a recording of The Armed Man by Karl Jenkins (1980). You can buy it on CD or look for a copy in the school or public library or ask the music department in your school for help. It is a musical depiction of what happens in a war. It brings together all nationalities and religions in a very moving way. It is surprisingly tuneful too.

- Research the history and work of the Red Cross which works in war zones and provides medical and other help for injured or needy people irrespective of which side they are on. The Red Crescent and the Red Crystal are non-Christian spin-offs. Find out about those too.

- You have probably heard of Florence Nightingale, but who was Mary Seacole and what did she achieve? Another interesting thing to look at in connection with the Crimean War (1853/6) is the writing of William Russell. Employed by *The Times*, he was effectively the first war correspondent because he was able to get same-day information back to London by telegraph.

READY FOR A REAL CHALLENGE?

David Jones (1895–1974) poet, water colourist and engraver served in the British army in France during the First World War. *In Parenthesis*, his highly praised long work – part poetry, part prose – based on his war experiences, was finally published in 1937. Study it and compare it with some of the better known World War One poetry. *In Parenthesis* is published by Faber & Faber or there are extracts in some anthologies.

Imagine you are in Antarctica and think about the penguin. Then let your mind wander to the huge ostrich of Africa – flightless like the penguin. Consider a tiny tropical humming bird no bigger than many an insect. Yes, there are birds in every country and every climate.

They come, all with feathers and beaks, in a dazzling array of colours, sizes and shapes – as David Attenborough's *The Life of Birds* (page 85) shows. So it isn't surprising that song birds, parrots, ducks, flamingos, owls, larks, cuckoos and the rest have always fascinated and inspired writers, poets and musicians.

Sadly, climate change and environmental damage means that some bird numbers are now dropping (even sparrows in Britain) and some are seriously endangered. In this chapter we consider birds – their beauty, habits, habitats and problems – from a range of points of view.

This chapter's title comes from a traditional nursery rhyme 'Who killed Cock Robin?' As you probably remember it goes like this: 'All the birds of the air fell a-sighing and a-sobbing when they heard of the death of poor Cock Robin.'

Passage A

1

5

This largely factual account of a study commissioned by the Royal Society for the Protection of Birds (RSPB) comes from a newspaper. The report sets out the dangers faced by birds in Britain and Europe as

10

temperatures rise. As you read it, notice how much of this passage is quoted or summarised from the study and how much is the journalist's own voice.

If you're a bird-lover and you want to see nesting snow buntings in the mountains of Scotland, or pintail ducks breeding in the fens of East Anglia, go now; their time here is limited. Research shows that British and European birds face a potentially disastrous future thanks to climate change during the coming century.

Three-quarters of the breeding birds of Britain and Europe are likely to decline in number as

15 the climatic range in which they can comfortably exist – their 'climate space' – shrinks with global warming, says a study by the Universities of Durham and Cambridge, in association with the Royal Society for the Protection of Birds (RSPB).

The picture is grim. With eight British breeding species, from the snow bunting and the pintail to the Scottish crossbill and the arctic skua, the shift is likely to mean
20 extinction by the century's end (or before) as the climate suitable for them ceases to exist in the British Isles.

With another group of similar size, including the red-throated diver and the dotterel, the distribution will shrink to a tiny fraction of the present range – less than five per cent – making the birds so rare they will be teetering on the edge of disappearance.

25 A third group of about 25 species, which includes many familiar waders, gulls and game birds, as well as woodland species, is also at risk. Its demise would shrink the British breeding range significantly; the birds are likely to vanish from many parts of the UK.

30 Thus redshanks, lapwings, curlews and snipe, all wading birds, are likely to cease nesting in all or most of southern England, as will common woodland birds such as the treecreeper. Red grouse, now bred and shot on moors in north Wales, northern England and Scotland, will probably vanish from the first two of these areas as the century progresses, and survive only north of the border.

35 The astonishingly detailed, species-by-species predictions are in a huge, innovative mapping project which outlines the future faced by 450 British and European bird species in a world of rising temperatures, published today as *A Climatic Atlas of European Breeding Birds*. The original and ingenious approach has been to work out the theoretical 'climate space', or 'climate envelope' in which each of the birds is able to flourish.

40 It is calculated using the parameters of how cold the winter is over its breeding range, how hot the summers are, and how much moisture is available. This is presented as a map. Then, using the supercomputer climate models which are the basis of present global warming predictions, the researchers have worked out how each species's climate space is likely to move as the warming takes hold over coming
45 decades, and the parameters defining it alter.

A new, and mostly dramatically different, series of maps shows that a typical bird's climate envelope shifts significantly by the end of the century from where it is today.

The remarkable conclusion is that, for the average bird species, the potential distribution by 2100 will shift nearly 550km (340 miles) north-east, equivalent to the
50 distance from Plymouth to Newcastle. And what follows is that the average European bird's distribution will be reduced by a fifth, and overlap its present range by only 40 per cent.

The predictions have been made with the main computer model of the global climate used by the Met Office's Hadley Centre for Climate Prediction and Research.
55 The basis has been a moderate scenario of future greenhouse gas emissions drawn up by the Intergovernmental Panel on Climate Change (IPCC), which suggests a rise in global average temperatures of just under three degrees C by the century's end.

The predictions for each species cannot be precise, because factors other than climate can ultimately determine range, such as habitat availability and direct efforts at
60 conservation. But the general thrust of this seven-year research project is crystal clear: the climate space available for 75 per cent of Europe's breeding birds is likely

to shrink, with their numbers consequently likely to decline in the worst cases to extinction. This dire conclusion has drawn calls for urgent action to combat climate change from the authors of the *Atlas*, Professors Brian Huntley, of Durham University,

65 and Rhys Green, of Cambridge University, and the RSPB, with Dr Yvonne Collingham and Dr Steve Willis, of Durham.

Professor Green said: 'Climatic change and wildlife's responses to it are difficult to forecast with any precision, but this study helps us to appreciate the magnitude and scope of possible impacts, and to identify species at most risk and those in need of

70 urgent help and protection.'

Mark Avery, the RSPB's director of conservation, added: 'We must heed the wake-up call and act immediately to curb climate change. Anything above an average of two degrees C risks catastrophic impacts for wildlife.'

Scotland is likely to be particularly hard-hit by the range shifts, with iconic Scottish

75 birds of mountain, forest and loch severely reduced in range and thus number. Six Scottish extinctions are forecast: snow bunting, Scottish crossbill, great skua and arctic skua, Leach's petrel and common scoter (a duck). The osprey, the fish-eating hawk which has returned to the Highlands in the past 50 years, is also predicted to vanish, but there is less confidence in this prediction because of difficulties in

80 mapping its present climate space correctly.

Some compensation for the potential losses may come in the shape of new birds colonising Britain from the Continent as their climate space shifts north. About 20 species fit into this category, each a British birdwatcher's dream, ranging from the serin, a small relative of the canary, to the spectacular cinnamon-coloured hoopoe,

85 and from the scops owl to the black kite.

But although the disappearance of a bird's 'climate space' from Britain is considered likely to lead to the disappearance of the species, there is no guarantee that the climate space of a species new to Britain will mean the birds will actually come here. We can only hope.

Slightly abridged from an article by the journalist Michael McCarthy,
The Independent, 15th January 2008

>> Task 5.1

1. What do scientists mean by 'climate space'? Use your own words.

2. Summarise in your own words what researchers believe will have happened to birds in Britain by 2100.

3. What, according to the experts, needs to be done to prevent the loss of bird species in Britain?

4. Explain how scientists have collected and presented their evidence.

Passage B

1   Sir David Attenborough is Britain's best-known naturalist. He began making popular and highly informative television

5   programmes in the 1950s and writing accompanying books. The Life of Birds was a major BBC series in the 1990s and this passage comes from the interesting, very

10   readable and beautifully illustrated book which went with it. Notice how Attenborough makes some quite complex science understandable for ordinary readers.

Birds' voices come from a structure that lies deep within their body, one that is possessed by no other creatures, called the syrinx.

This box-shaped organ, strengthened around the outside with hoops of cartilage, lies at the bottom end of the bird's windpipe where that divides into the two tubes which lead to its pair of lungs. Within the syrinx, each of these tubes can be closed completely or partially by a pair of fleshy lips. When the bird contracts

15   its lungs, a jet of air is blown through each pair, creating a musical sound. Muscles within the syrinx enable a bird to vibrate each pair of lips independently and so vary the pitch and quality of the note which comes from each.

20   The windpipe up which the notes then travel also modifies them. As with the pipe of an organ, the longer the windpipe, the deeper the sounds it emits as the air in it resonates. Cranes, which produce trombone-like calls, have windpipes that are so long that they curl into loops alongside the keel of their breastbones, and in some cases pass right through it. One of the plainer birds of paradise, the trumpet bird,

25   has one that runs down across its chest just beneath the surface of the skin and forms a loop. As a trumpet bird gets older so it develops more loops. Only the males

have them and only the males produce the organ-like trumpeting calls that give the species its name – though considering the lavish looping of its windpipe, it might have been more appropriate to call it the French horn bird.

30   Some birds are able at will to shorten their windpipes. Like the syrinx, the windpipe is encircled by strengthening rings of cartilage. These are connected to one another by muscles which enable the bird to pull the rings closer to one another like the pleats of a closing concertina. As that happens so the resonances from the windpipe rise in pitch. Penguins have a partition running the length of their windpipe, dividing

35   it into two equal halves, so when the jackass penguin brays – it can hardly be said to sing – it produces a two-note chord.

By taking shallow mini-breaths, accurately co-ordinated with the notes of its call, a bird can sing without a noticeable break in the sound for minutes on end, far longer than even the most highly-trained human singer is able to do. Each pair of lips within

40   the syrinx may produce its own sound. Canaries, when trilling, create 90% of the sound with the left tube and use the right mainly for breathing. Cardinals, whistling a glissando, start the lower section with one tube and mix through imperceptibly to the other tube for the higher half. The two sounds from the two tubes may also combine and interact with one another to create a quite different sound. This explains how

45   some birds, such as parrots and mynahs, are able to produce eerily close imitations of human speech, even though they lack the lips and variable mobile tongue with which humans make such sounds. All in all, in duration, variety and complexity, no other vocalisations produced by any other animal can match the song of a bird.

From *The Life of Birds* by David Attenborough (1998)

>> Task 5.2

1. What is the syrinx and how does it work?

2. In which two ways, according to this passage, are birds different from any other animal?

3. Summarise in your own words the functions of a bird's windpipe.

4. Passages A and B are both examples of factual, scientific writing in which the technical information is presented in a way that allows readers, untrained as scientists, to understand it. What do the two passages have in common and how do they differ?

Passage C

Gerald Durrell (1925-1995) was ahead of his time in being very worried about endangered species almost from boyhood. Eventually he founded a conservation centre in Jersey which is now at the cutting edge of international efforts to save endangered species. Part of his early work involved travelling the world to collect the rare species to breed from back in Jersey. At the same time he wrote witty, best-selling books about his adventures. At first, it was the profits from these which funded much of his work. The Drunken Forest is about a collecting trip to Argentina and Paraguay. In this extract he shares his impressions of a newly captured creature - a screamer bird. He describes the bird almost as if it was human - a technique known as anthropomorphism. Do you find it effective or irritating?

Eggbert's feet were the bane of his life. There was so much of them, and they would get tangled together when he walked. Then there was the danger that he would tread on his own toes and fall down and make an exhibition of himself, as he had done on the first day. So he kept a very close watch on his feet for any signs of insubordination. He would sometimes stand for as long as ten minutes with head bent, gravely staring at his toes as they wiggled gently in the grass, spread out like the arms of a starfish. Eggbert's whole desire, obviously, was to be disassociated from these outsize feet. He felt irritated by them. Without them, he was sure, he could gambol about the lawn with the airy grace of a dried thistle-head. Occasionally, having watched his feet for some time, he would decide that he had lulled them into a sense of false security. Then, when they least suspected it, he would launch his body forward in an effort to speed across the lawn and leave these hateful extremities behind. But although he tried this trick many times, it never succeeded. The feet were always too quick for him, and as soon as he moved they would deliberately and maliciously twist themselves into a knot, and Eggbert would fall head first into the daisies.

His feet were continually letting him down in more ways than one. Eggbert had a deep ambition to capture a butterfly. Why this was we could not find out, for Eggbert could not tell us. All we knew was that screamers were supposed to be entirely vegetarian, but whenever a butterfly hovered within six feet of Eggbert his whole being seemed to be filled with blood-lust. His eyes would take on a most un-vegetarian-like gleam, and he would endeavour to stalk it. However, in order to stalk a butterfly with any hope of success one has to keep one's eyes firmly fixed on it. This Eggbert knew, but the trouble was that as soon as he watched the butterfly

Screamer bird

45 with quivering concentration, his feet, left to their own devices, would start to play up, treading on each other's toes, crossing over each other, and sometimes even trying to walk in the wrong directions. As soon as Eggbert dragged his eyes away from the quarry, his feet would start to behave, but by the time he looked back again the butterfly would have disappeared.

From *The Drunken Forest* by Gerald Durrell (1956)

▶▶ Task 5.3

1. What, according to the writer, seems to be the problem with Eggbert's feet? Explain in your own words.

   _____

2. Explain why the writer is intrigued by Eggbert's interest in the butterfly.

   _____

3. Choose and write about three phrases which you particularly like or find interesting.

   _____

4. What do we learn from this passage about the writer?

Passage D

Ted Hughes, a Yorkshireman whose first wife was the American poet Sylvia Plath, was one of the 20th century's most highly regarded poets. He often wrote about birds and animals but there was absolutely nothing sentimental about his views. 'Thrushes' is an early poem and one of Hughes's best known. Thrushes are not kind. They are not human. No emotion or empathy controls their actions. The poet marvels at their efficiency. Hughes had a great gift for presenting life exactly as it is.

Thrushes

1   Terrifying are the attent sleek thrushes on the lawn,
More coiled steel than living—a poised
Dark deadly eye, those delicate legs
Triggered to stirrings beyond sense—with a start, a bounce, a stab
5   Overtake the instant and drag out some writhing thing.
No indolent procrastinations and no yawning stares,
No sighs or head-scratchings. Nothing but bounce and stab
And a ravening second.

Is it their single-mind-sized skulls, or a trained
10   Body, or genius, or a nestful of brats
Gives their days this bullet and automatic
Purpose? Mozart's brain had it, and the shark's mouth
That hungers down the blood-smell even to a leak of its own
Side and devouring of itself: efficiency which
15   Strikes too streamlined for any doubt to pluck at it
Or obstruction deflect.

With a man it is otherwise. Heroisms on horseback,
Outstripping his desk-diary at a broad desk,
Carving at a tiny ivory ornament
20   For years: his act worships itself—while for him,
Though he bends to be blent in the prayer, how loud and above what
Furious spaces of fire do the distracting devils
Orgy and hosannah, under what wilderness
Or black silent waters weep.

'Thrushes' by Ted Hughes (1960)

Passage E

Laurie Lee was a countryman with an artist's eye for observation as this descriptive, colourful poem shows. Lee was born in the Cotswolds but travelled widely – notably to Spain to fight against Franco in the 1930s (see note in the 'Wide Range Reading' section of Chapter 4) about which he wrote several books. He described his childhood too in a famous book called Cider with Rosie (1959).

Cock-pheasant

1 Gilded with leaf-thick paint; a steady
Eye fixed like a ruby rock;
Across the cidrous banks of autumn
Swaggers the stamping pheasant-cock.

5 The thrusting nut and bursting apple
Accompany his jointed walk,
The creviced pumpkin and the marrow
Bend to his path on melting stalk.

Sure as an Inca priest or devil,
10 Feathers stroking down the corn,
He blinks the lively dust of daylight,
Blind to the hunter's powder-horn.

For me, alike, this flushed October—
Ripe, and round-fleshed, and bellyful—
15 Fevers me fast but cannot fright, though
Each dropped leaf shows the winter's skull.

'Cock-pheasant' by Laurie Lee

⟩⟩ Task 5.4

1. In Passage D what does the poet mean by 'No indolent procrastinations and no yawning stares' (line 6)? Answer in as much detail as you can using short quotations from the poem (enclosed in inverted commas) in your sentences.

2. Choose three examples from Passage E of the poet's drawing our attention to sights, sounds, smells, tastes and sensations and write about each as fully as you can.

3. Which poem do you prefer and why? You might like to comment on:

   • each poet's ideas

   • the effectiveness of comparisons such as metaphors and similes

   • the sound of the words in each poem and the way they are grouped

   • each poet's use of rhyme and rhythm.

Writing about literature

Here is an example, focused on lines 22 to 29 in Passage B, of how you might comment in detail on the language and style of non-fiction writing.

Attenborough's use of non-technical language ('chest' 'loop') makes the meaning of this passage very clear for mainstream readers. On the whole he avoids long words derived from Latin too and chooses short, plain verbs such as 'runs', 'gets' and 'have'. And the sentence structure is often straightforward. The sentence beginning 'As a trumpet bird gets …' is a compound of two simple statements (The bird gets older. It develops more loops.) and contains only 11 words. All of this adds to clarity. The repetition of 'only' in the third sentence emphasises the trumpet bird's unusualness and the French horn joke at the end of the paragraph lightens the tone because this text was written for mass informative entertainment rather than as a paper for other scientists. There is also an easy elegance about this language reinforced by alliterative phrases such as 'plainer birds of paradise' and 'lavish looping'.

⟩⟩ Task 5.5

Choose a few lines from Passage A or Passage B and write a paragraph commenting on them in detail.

Personal Writing

>> Task 5.6

1. Think of a bird (or other animal) you know well or have observed closely and write a humorous description of its antics.

2. Write a bird poem. Choose your own style.

3. Research the dodo and its destruction. Write a factual account of the bird and its fate. Be objective and do not include your own views.

4. Write a story, poem, article, essay – or any other piece of writing you choose – using the title 'The Eagle and the Wren'.

5. Write an article for a children's reference book explaining how birds fly. You will need to research the subject first and it may help you to discuss this with a partner and to co-write the piece.

6. Write about birds in any way you wish.

Writing tip

When you write factually for the purpose of explaining something to someone:

• never use a long word where a short one will do

• keep your sentences as concise as you can

• don't 'decorate' your work with unnecessary adjectives and adverbs

• if you can find an analogy or comparison (e.g. Attenborough's likening the trumpet-bird's looped windpipe to a French horn) to help you explain then use it

• edit your work several times. Each time you come back to it you will probably see other ways of 'tightening' and improving it.

WORD BANK

Michael McCarthy uses the word **consequently** which comes from *sequor* the Latin meaning I follow.

He also uses **magnitude** – from the Latin adjective *magnus* meaning great.

The word **catastrophic**, also used in Passage A, is an adjective deriving from the Greek noun *katastrophe*. Its literal meaning is **overturning** from *cata* (down, away, off, against) and *strephein* (to turn).

Interestingly the word **apostrophe** comes from the same root. As well as being a punctuation mark it is also a digression in speaking or writing – a turning away.

>> Task 5.7

Give definitions for the following words each of which shares a root with one of the three words mentioned above:

1. cataclysm
2. magnification
3. magnum
4. sequacious

5. cataplexy
6. sequential
7. magniloquent
8. obsequious

>> Task 5.8

Use these words, all taken from the five passages in this chapter, in sentences of your own to show that you understand their meaning.

1. swaggers
2. emits
3. potentially
4. iconic
5. bane

6. resonates
7. teetering
8. keel
9. cidrous
10. demise

11. deflect
12. innovative
13. maliciously
14. attent
15. parameters

>> Task 5.9

Study the spellings in this passage taken from the final paragraph in Passage A. Working with a partner, take it in turns to dictate this section to each other. Check your work with this book. Relearn the spellings of any words you got wrong.

> But although the disappearance of a bird's 'climate space' from Britain is considered likely to lead to the disappearance of the species, there is no guarantee that the climate space of a species new to Britain will mean the birds will actually come here. We can only hope.

NUTS AND BOLTS

Direct and indirect speech

There are two main ways of telling a reader what someone has said.

You can use direct speech like this:

> Professor Green said: 'Climatic change and wildlife's responses to it are difficult to forecast with any precision, but this study helps us to appreciate the magnitude and scope of possible impacts, and to identify species at most risk and those in need of urgent help and protection.'
>
> Mark Avery, the RSPB's director of conservation, added: 'We must heed the wake-up call and act immediately to curb climate change. Anything above an average of two degrees C risks catastrophic impacts for wildlife.'

Or indirect speech like this:

> Professor Green explained that climatic change and wildlife's responses to it are difficult to forecast with any precision. But he argues that this study helps scientists to appreciate the magnitude and scope of possible impacts, and to identify species at most risk and those in need of urgent help and protection.
>
> Mark Avery, the RSPB's director of conservation, agrees. He wants people to heed the wake-up call and act immediately to curb climate change. He believes that anything above an average of two degrees C risks catastrophic impacts for wildlife.

In the first example the writer gives you the exact words spoken. He 'quotes' them. These quotations are enclosed in inverted commas (sometimes called 'quotation marks') to make it clear that they are precise. In a sense it is as if the speakers are in a play and these are their lines.

In the second example the writer has summarised – paraphrased or reported – what Professor Green and Mark Avery said without quoting them directly. Indirect speech is sometimes called reported speech.

Most fiction writers use a mixture to keep dialogue flowing and interesting. Look at this passage from Anna Sewell's *Black Beauty* (1877). Can you work out which is which?

> Two days after the accident, Blantyre paid me a visit; he patted me and praised me very much. He told Lord George that he was sure the horse knew of Annie's danger as well as he did. 'I could not have held him in if I would', said he; 'she ought never to ride any other horse.' I found out by their conversation that my young mistress was now out of danger and would soon be able to ride again. This was good news to me and I looked forward to a happy life.

Notice that in indirect/reported speech:

- verbs such as **explained**, **argued** and **told** (us) are used rather than the direct **said**, **shouted**, **whispered** and so on

- because it is, in effect, a summary the text is often shorter than it would be if every word is set down exactly as it was (or would be) spoken.

>> Task 5.10

Plays' texts, of course, always consist of direct speech because the playwright writes exactly what he or she wants the actors to say.

Rewrite this short extract from *You Made Me* by Kelvin Reynolds and Adrian Lockwood (Collins Play Plus) in a mixture of direct and indirect speech as if it were in a novel or story.

> *Kelly is packing her bag, Lucy tries to remove the headphones on the table from the personal stereo.*
>
> KELLY: Hey, leave them alone. *(snatching them back)*
>
> LUCY: These are mine. Look they've got a blue mark on.
>
> KELLY: You've broken yours. You know you have.
>
> LUCY: Give them back now! *(Lucy tries to pull them away but Kelly puts them in her bag)*
>
> KELLY: *(triumphantly)* They're mine.
>
> LUCY: I hate you!
>
> KELLY: Just go away will you?
>
> LUCY: It's not fair. You've already got two pairs and I haven't got any. *(Lucy storms off)*
>
> KELLY: *(to audience)* Little sisters. Such a pain. But she's right of course.

Be careful with less, few and fewer.

Less refers to quantity. So you can write less science, less rainfall and less hope.

Fewer or few refer to number. So it should be fewer sparrows, few eagles, few ornithologists.

A quick way of remembering this is that if it's something you can count (sparrows, eagles, ornithologists) it is 'few' or 'fewer'. If you can't count whatever it is use 'less'. (One or two British supermarkets have a notice saying 'Baskets containing fewer than eight items' – which is correct. Several other supermarkets get this wrong. Watch out for it.)

>> Task 5.11

Put less, fewer, few into the gaps in these sentences:

1. There are ... finches in British gardens than there used to be.

2. ... pollution would probably mean ... losses of bird species.

3. ... scientists ignore global warming.

4. ... speed on the roads would result in ... accidents.

5. Small birds need ... space to take off than large ones.

6. There are now so ... places to smoke in that ... people are buying cigarettes so there is much ... friction between smokers and non-smokers.

Use the word **literally** with great care. It means **absolutely** and **physically true**. It doesn't mean 'very'.

So to write 'I was literally bursting with excitement when I heard that an osprey was nesting nearby' is nonsense because you were not actually bursting. It is a metaphor. You were simply very excited.

On the other hand if you say 'She was literally speechless when she heard she had won the prize so her Dad had to thank the judges on her behalf', you really do mean that she was unable to speak – so literally is correct.

Use **literally** for emphasis when one would normally expect something to be metaphorically, but not literally, true. For example: 'She was literally glued to her chair because my naughty little brother had spilled some paste there and not bothered to clear it up'.

>> Task 5.12

Write six sentences of your own in which you use 'literally' correctly.

All the Birds of the Air **5**

More speaking and listening activities

Watch one episode of David Attenborough's *Life of Birds* (or one of his other series – all are available on DVD to buy or through libraries). Listen very carefully to the sound track. At the end write a two-paragraph summary of what you have learned.

Read one or more of the books listed in the 'Wide Range Reading' section of this chapter. Then talk about it to a small group or to the class.

Work in a pair. Tell each other an anecdote about an occasion when you have encountered a bird (in the garden, at a zoo, on holiday, in an aviary, in a cage in someone's sitting room, at the seaside or whatever). Listen carefully to each other. Then team up with another pair. Take it in turns to tell the other two your partner's (not your own) anecdote.

Organise a group discussion or debate about global warming and its effect on birds. There is some information in Passage A but you will need to collect more. RSPB is a useful resource. See www.rspb.org.uk. Another is Durrell Wildlife Conservation Trust www.durrellwildlife.org.

Eliminate two words from the list for each of the clues. The word left over when all the clues are solved is the answer to the puzzle.

Here are two examples of how the clues work:

clue: two to go with book
answer: **cookery** and **jacket** (cookery book and book jacket)

clue: two to go with desk
answer: **school** and **drawer** (school desk and desk drawer)

window	arch	glove	suspension
guide	ash	cleaner	capital
racing	red	work	suit

phone	loss	road
collar	boot	post
fishing	spare	house

1. Two to go with bridge
2. Two to go with car
3. Two to go with tree
4. Two to go with carpet
5. Two to go with city
6. Two to go with shop
7. Two to go with net
8. Two to go with wheel
9. Two to go with dog
10. Two to go with sign

WIDE RANGE READING

Life in Cold Blood by David Attenborough (2008) is a marvellous book about reptiles based on the big 2008 TV series (now available on DVD) of the same title. Given the author's age this will probably be his last major TV series and book since his work has always involved travelling to remote parts of many countries worldwide to observe and film. My A Level zoology (study of animals) teacher taught me that birds and reptiles have a lot in common. She argued that, in some ways, birds are reptiles with feathers and reptiles are birds with scales. Read this book and see whether you agree with her.

Golden Bats and Pink Pigeons by Gerald Durrell (1977) is an entertaining account of the author's collecting trip to Mauritius to rescue endangered animals including the pink pigeons of the title and Mauritian kestrels. Now independent, the island, which is in the Indian Ocean, east of Madagascar, was a French colony until 1715 when it was seized by the British. It has some of the world's rarest plants and animals. The dodo – now the very appropriate logo for the Durrell centre in Jersey – was hunted to extinction there in the eighteenth century by European settlers.

The Birds and Other Stories by Daphne Du Maurier (1952). Walking near her home in Cornwall the author saw a farmer busily ploughing a field. Above him were seagulls diving and wheeling. From this she developed the powerful idea for the lead story in this book. In it, the birds become hostile after a harsh winter with little food. First the seagulls, then birds of prey and finally even small birds turn against mankind. The nightmarish idea appealed to film director Alfred Hitchcock who turned it into a celebrated film (1953). The other stories in the book are worth reading too.

Cranes Flying South by N Karazin (1931). This is an unusual minor classic which tells the story of cranes migrating in a huge group. They are escaping the cold winter in Russia and heading for the warmth of Africa as thousands of birds do every year. The story literally gives the reader a 'bird's eye view'. It is told by a young crane and is strong on the length of the journey, the geography of the land they fly over and problems like fatigue and feeding.

The Bedside Book of Birds: An Avian Miscellany edited by Graeme Gibson (2007). This is an attractive selection of writings about birds from various genres. It includes scientific observation, reflections, poetry and fiction. Classic writers represented include Shakespeare and Coleridge alongside more recent ones such as Ted Hughes and Bruce Chatwin. It's a splendid 'dipping' book which shows how birds have inspired and affected human beings in many different ways for hundreds of years.

Don't forget to look in anthologies for poems about birds too. As well as other poems by Ted Hughes and Laurie Lee look for work by DH Lawrence, Alfred Lord Tennyson, Emily Dickinson, Andrew Young and Seamus Heaney – among many others.

- **Bird song has inspired many composers to try to imitate it in their music. Listen, for example, to The Lark Ascending by Ralph Vaughan Williams. Decide how well you think the music evokes the bird. You could then try The Birds by Ottorino Respighi or Ludwig van Beethoven's sixth symphony.**

- **Choose a bird which really interests you – from anywhere in the world. Find out about its appearance, food, breeding habits, habitat, endangered status (if it is at risk) and so on. Create an illustrated poster for the classroom wall summing up the information.**

- **Read the passage from *Bleak House* by Charles Dickens when Miss Flite is introduced (Chapter 5 – about two thirds of the way through beginning 'She lived at the top of the house …'). She is an eccentric surrounded by caged birds.**

Study the symbolism of birds. In art and religion specific birds often stand for a quality or emotion – and/or they carry some sort of message. Their presence in logos and as national emblems – such as the mighty eagle of Ancient Rome or the USA – is significant too. Find out the traditional meanings of birds such as the dove, nightingale, raven, swan and others. A good art dictionary or a dictionary of symbolism will help you.

6 The World at Work

What do you understand by 'work'? Is it what you have to do at school in order to make progress and pass your exams? Is it what your teachers and others employed at your school do? Or is it something people go off and do in offices or workshops. What about me? As I type these words for you to read, am I working? What about a parent looking after a young child at home?

The truth is, of course, that work is all of those and many more. It's a big 'umbrella' term. It covers anything which people have to do during an ordinary day, whether it's part of education, to do with running family life, or a way of earning money. Whether you use your hands, your skills, your brain or your pen, or a combination of those and other things too, it is all work.

To begin this chapter I have gathered together writings about several different sorts of manual work in the past – from toiling in the fields to providing public transport. Some are fiction. One is reportage and two are poems.

Passage A

In his most famous novel, Tess of the D'Urbervilles (1891), Thomas Hardy tells the tragic story of Tess, 'a pure woman'. From a poor family, Tess finds herself obliged to become involved with an unworthy but wealthy man who doesn't love her nor she him. Later, while working on a dairy farm, she meets another man with whom she falls deeply in love. But it goes horribly wrong when, at last, she tells him about her past. At the point in the novel from which this passage comes she is at a very low ebb working as a hired hand on a farm with other women. Notice how fully Hardy describes the threshing process and the gruelling work it involves.

The rick was unhaled by full daylight; the men then took their places, the women mounted, and the work began. Farmer Groby – or, as they called him, 'he' – had arrived ere this, and by his orders Tess was placed on a platform of the machine, close to the men who fed it, her business being to untie every sheaf of corn handed on to her by Izz Huett, who stood next, but on the rick; so that the feeder could seize and spread it over the revolving drum, which whisked out every grain in one moment.

They were soon in full progress, after a preparatory hitch or two, which rejoiced the hearts of those who hated machinery. The work sped on till breakfast-time, when the thresher was stopped for half an hour; and, on starting again after the meal, the whole supplementary strength of the farm was thrown into the labour of constructing the straw-rick, which began to grow beside the stack of corn. A hasty lunch was eaten as they stood, without leaving their

100

30 positions, and then another couple of hours brought them near to dinner-time; the inexorable wheels continuing to spin, and the penetrating hum of the thresher to thrill to the very marrow all who were near to the revolving wire-cage.

35 Old men on the rising straw-rick talked of the past days when they had been accustomed to thresh with flails on the oaken barn-floor; when everything, even to winnowing, was effected by hand-labour, which, to their thinking, though 40 slow, produced better results. Those, too, on the corn-rick talked a little; but the

The Threshing Machine by Edmond Charles Yon (1836-97)

perspiring ones at the machine, including Tess, could not lighten their duties by the exchange of many words. It was the ceaselessness of the work which tried her so severely, and began to make her wish that she had never come to Flintcomb-Ash. The 45 women on the corn-rick – Marian, who was one of them, in particular – could stop to drink ale or cold tea from the flagon now and then, or to exchange a few gossiping remarks while they wiped their faces or cleared the fragments of straw and husk from their clothing; but for Tess there was no respite; for, as the drum never stopped, the man who fed it could not stop either, unless Marian changed places with her, 50 which she sometimes did for half an hour in spite of Groby's objection that she was too slow-handed for a feeder.

For some probably economical reason it was usually a woman who was chosen for this particular duty, and Groby gave as his motive in selecting Tess that she was one of those who combined strength with quickness in untying, and both with staying 55 power, and this may have been true. The hum of the thresher, which prevented speech, increased to a raving whenever the supply of corn fell short of the regular quantity. As Tess and the man who fed could never turn their heads she did not know that just before the dinner-hour a person had come silently into the field by the gate, and had been standing under a second rick watching the scene, and Tess in 60 particular. He was dressed in a tweed suit of fashionable pattern, and he twirled a gay walking-cane.

'Who is that?' said Izz Huett to Marian. She had at first addressed the enquiry to Tess, but the latter could not hear it.

'Somebody's fancy man, I s'pose', said Marian laconically.

65 'I'll lay a guinea he's after Tess.'

From *Tess of the D'Urbervilles* by Thomas Hardy (1891)

>> Task 6.1

1. Explain in your own words Tess's exact job in the threshing process.

2. What can you deduce from this passage about 19th century farming and how it was changing? Answer in as much detail as you can.

3. What do you learn about Tess herself from this extract?

Passage B

Thomas Hardy was both a poet and novelist. He wrote a whole string of novels between 1871 and 1895 finishing with Jude the Obscure. Some people said this novel was immoral because a couple in it live together happily (for a while) and have children without being married. So upset was Hardy by the criticism of Jude the Obscure that he vowed that from then on he would write only poetry. He lived another 33 years. So he is, in effect, a nineteenth century novelist and a twentieth century poet. In either genre he always expressed love of nature and tradition and hatred of change as this poem shows.

Throwing a Tree

1
The two executioners stalk along over the knolls,
Bearing two axes with heavy heads shining and wide,
And a long limp two-handled saw toothed for cutting great boles,
And so they approach the proud tree that bears the death-mark on its side.

5
Jackets doffed they swing axes and chop away just above ground,
And chips fly about and lie white on moss and fallen leaves;
Till a broad deep gash in the bark is hewn all the way round,
And one of them tries to hook upward a rope, which at last he achieves.

The saw then begins, till the top of the tall giant shivers:
10
The shivers are seen to grow greater each cut than before:
They edge out the saw, tug the rope; but the tree only quivers,
And kneeling and sawing again, they step back to try pulling once more.

15

Then, lastly, the living mast sways, further sways: with a shout
Job and Ike rush aside. Reached the end of its long staying powers
The tree crashes downward: it shakes all its neighbours throughout,
And two hundred years' steady growth has been ended in less than two hours.

'Throwing a Tree' by Thomas Hardy (1927)

Task 6.2

1a. In what sense are the tree-fellers 'executioners'?

b. How does Hardy reinforce this comparison as the poem continues? Answer in as much detail as you can and weave short quotations (enclosed in inverted commas) into your sentences.

2. What does Hardy's use of rhyme add to the poem? Look closely at details such as:

   • the links in meaning between rhyming words

   • rhymes and half rhymes within lines (technically known as 'internal rhyme')

   • the effect of the rhyme on the poem's rhythm. Are the rhythmic sounds linked to what Hardy is describing?

3. Choose three phrases or lines which you found interesting and write about them in detail.

4. What do these two pieces of Hardy – Passages A and B – have in common? Look at the language, the descriptions and the things which seem to interest Hardy most.

Passage C

Chinua Achebe is Nigeria's best-known writer. He won the Nobel Prize for Literature in 2006. In his most famous and magnificently well-written book he shows us the traditional life of Nigeria's country people and how it was ruined by the arrival and interference of white settlers from Britain and elsewhere wanting to impose Christianity on the Ibo people. 'Things Fall Apart' - a quotation from the Irish poet, W B Yeats - is for Achebe an accurate summary of what happened to his fellow Nigerians in the nineteenth century. In this passage the main character, Okonkwo, is struggling in difficult circumstances to grow food. His 'inflexible will' will soon get him into trouble.

The year that Okonkwo took eight hundred seed-yams from Nwakibie was the worst year in living memory. Nothing happened at its proper time; it was either too early or too late. It seemed as if the world had gone mad. The first rains were late, and, when they came, lasted only a brief moment. The blazing sun returned, more fierce than it had ever been known, and scorched all the green that had appeared with the rains. The earth burned like hot coals and roasted all the yams that had been sown. Like all good farmers, Okonkwo had begun to sow with the first rains. He had sown four hundred seeds when the rain dried up and the heat returned. He watched the sky all day for signs of rain-clouds and lay awake all night. In the morning he went back to his farm and saw the withering tendrils. He had tried to protect them from the smouldering earth by making rings of thick sisal leaves around them. But by the end of the day the sisal rings were burnt dry and grey. He changed them every day, and prayed that the rain might fall in the night. But the drought continued for eight market weeks and the yams were killed.

Some farmers had not planted their yams yet. They were the lazy easy-going ones who always put off clearing their farms as long as they could. This year they were the wise ones. They sympathised with their neighbours with much shaking of the head, but inwardly they were happy for what they took to be their own foresight.

Okonkwo planted what was left of his seed-yams when the rains finally returned. He had one consolation. The yams he had sown before the drought were his own, the harvest of the previous year. He still had the eight hundred from Nwakibie and the four hundred from his father's friend. So he would make a fresh start.

But the year had gone mad. Rain fell as it has never fallen before. For days and nights together it poured down in violent torrents, and washed away the yam heaps.

Trees were uprooted and deep gorges appeared everywhere. Then the rain became less violent. But it went on from day to day without pause. The spell of sunshine which always came in the middle of the wet season did not appear. The yams put on luxuriant green leaves, but every farmer knew that without sunshine the tubers would not grow.

45

That year the harvest was sad, like a funeral, and many farmers wept as they dug up the miserable and rotting yams. One man tied his cloth to the branch of a tree and hanged himself.

Okonkwo remembered that tragic year with a cold shiver throughout the rest of his life. It always surprised him when he thought of it later that he did not sink under the load of despair. He knew that he was a fierce fighter, but that year had been enough to break the heart of a lion.

50

'Since I survived that year', he always said, 'I shall survive anything.' He put it down to his inflexible will.

From *Things Fall Apart* by Chinua Achebe (1958)

>> Task 6.3

1. What does this passage teach about traditional African farming?

2. Summarise in a single paragraph the problems faced by Okonkwo and other farmers 'that year'.

3. Although these passages were written 70 years apart, Passage A and Passage C are describing farming at about the same time in the 19th century. List the differences.

4. How does Achebe's style differ from Hardy's (prose) style? Look at vocabulary, sentence length and shape and punctuation (including paragraphing). Answer in as much detail as you can.

Like Hardy - with whom he is often compared - DH Lawrence was a fine poet as well as novelist, short story and travel writer (see the extract from one of his short stories in Chapter 2 on page 23). In this short poem he finds real beauty in a simple scene of railway track workers in the rain. Once you have read and thought about this poem you will probably not be surprised to learn that Lawrence was also a keen - and quite competent - painter.

Morning Work

1   A gang of labourers on the wet piled timber
    That shines blood-red beside the railway siding
    Seem to be making out of the blue of the morning
    Something faery and fine, the shuttles sliding.

5   The red-gold spools of their hands and their faces swinging
    Hither and thither across the high crystalline frame
    Of day: trolls at the cave of ringing cerulian mining
    And laughing with labour, living their work like a game.

'Morning Work' by DH Lawrence (1913)

>>Task 6.4

Write a short essay comparing Passage D with Passage B. Consider:

- the poets' attitude to the workers they describe
- the extent to which the two poets approve of the work they are observing
- the use of imagery (metaphors, similes and personification) and what it adds
- the effect of any other poetic techniques such as rhyme and alliteration.

Passage E

This passage comes from a modern novel set in 17th century Delft in the Netherlands where many artists lived and worked. The narrator is the daughter of a tile-maker (Delft was, and is, famous for decorative tiles) who is working as a maid in the household of Johannes Vermeer. A well-known painting by Vermeer, known as The Girl with the Pearl Earring, hangs today in a gallery in The Hague. Tracy Chevalier's novel plays with the idea that a fictional maid was the model for the painting and that she became very close to the artist. Here 'the girl' enters her master's studio for the first time. Dutch paintings of this period are remarkable for their observation of everyday domestic detail. Chevalier is imitating that here. In a sense she is painting with words.

I opened the lower window and shutters and got down from the chair. Something moved in front of me and I froze. The movement stopped. It was me, reflected in a mirror that hung on the wall between the two windows. I gazed at myself. Although I had an anxious, guilty expression, my face was also bathed in light, making my skin glow. I stared, surprised, then stepped away.

Now that I had a moment I surveyed the room. It was a large, square space, not as long as the great hall downstairs. With the windows open it was bright and airy, with whitewashed walls, and grey and white marble tiles on the floor, the darker tiles set in a pattern of square crosses. A row of Delft tiles painted with cupids lined the bottom of the walls to protect the whitewash from our mops. They were not my father's.

Though it was a big room, it held little furniture. There was the easel and chair in front of the window in the right corner. Beside the chair I had stood on there was another by the table, of plain leather nailed on with brass studs, and two lion heads carved into the tops of the posts. Against the far wall, behind the chair and easel, was a small cupboard, its drawers closed, several brushes and a knife with a diamond-shaped blade arranged on top to clean palettes. Beside the cupboard was a desk on which were papers, books and prints. Two more lion-headed chairs had been set against the wall near the doorway.

It was an orderly room, empty of the clutter of everyday life. It felt different from the rest of the house, almost as if it were in a different house altogether. When the door was closed it would be difficult to hear the shouts of the children, the jangle of Catherina's keys, the sweeping of our brooms.

I took up my broom, bucket of water and dustcloth and began to clean. I started in the corner where the scene of the painting had been set up, where I knew I

45 must not move a thing. I kneeled on the chair to dust the window I had struggled to open, and the yellow curtain that hung to one side in the corner, touching it lightly so that I would not disturb its folds.

50 The panes of glass were dirty and needed scrubbing with warm water, but I was not sure if he wanted them clean. I would have to ask Catherina.

I dusted the chairs, polishing the brass

55 studs and lion heads. The table had not been cleaned properly in some time. Someone had wiped around the objects placed there – a powderbrush, a pewter bowl, a letter, a black ceramic pot, blue

60 cloth heaped to one side and hanging over the edge – but they had to be moved for the table really to be cleaned. As my mother had said, I would have to find a way to move things yet put them back

65 exactly as if they had not been touched.

Girl with a Pearl Earring by Vermeer, c1665

From *Girl with a Pearl Earring* by Tracy Chevalier (1999)

>> Task 6.5

1. Summarise what you learn about the narrator from this passage.

2. Compare Chevalier's style with Achebe's (Passage C) and Hardy's in Passage A.

Passage F

1   Henry Mayhew (1812–1887) was an investigative journalist. He focused on the lives of ordinary people in mid-19th century
5   London - the ones who were poor or who had to work very hard in unpleasant, low-paid jobs. He spent months on the streets observing and interviewing. He published his findings in a series of 82 newspaper
10 articles which eventually became the book from which this extract comes. Mayhew's work was important because many newspaper readers were well off and had
15 no idea what street life was like. He wanted sympathy and understanding for the poor. For us, today, Mayhew's writing is valuable
20 because it is so detailed. There is a great deal about Victorian London which would have been lost had Mayhew not recorded it. His work has provided source material for
25 many a historical novelist, for example.

Omnibus Conductors

The conductor, who is vulgarly known as the 'cad', stands on a small projection at the end of the omnibus; and it is his office to admit and set down every passenger, and to receive the amount of fare, for which amount he is, of course, responsible to his employers. He is paid 4s (20p) a-day, which he is allowed to stop out of the monies he receives. He fills up a waybill each journey, with the number of passengers. I find that nearly all classes have given a quota of their number to the list of conductors. Among them are grocers, drapers, shopmen, barmen, printers, tailors, shoe-makers, clerks, joiners, saddlers, coach-builders, porters, town-travellers, carriers, and fish-mongers. Unlike the drivers, the majority of conductors are unmarried men; but, perhaps, only a mere majority. As

a matter of necessity every conductor must be able to read and write. They are discharged more frequently than the drivers; but they require good characters before
30 their appointment. From one of them, a very intelligent man, I had the following statement:-

'I am 35 or 36, and have been a conductor for six years. Before that I was a lawyer's clerk, and then a picture-dealer; but didn't get on, though I maintained a good character. I'm a conductor now, but wouldn't be long behind a 'bus if it wasn't from
35 necessity. It's hard to get anything else to do that can keep a wife and family on, for people won't have you from off a 'bus. The worst part of my business is its uncertainty, I may be discharged any day, and not know for what.'

From *London Labour and the London Poor* by Henry Mayhew (1850)

Horse drawn omnibus with passengers, London, c1905

>> Task 6.6

Working with a partner compare this passage with any of the prose passages above. Remember in your discussion that Passages A, C and E are fiction. Passage F is a factual report. So there are differences but there are also similarities. Look together at the writing style as well as the meaning.

Writing about literature

Study this short example of writing about poetry which compares DH Lawrence's 'Morning Work' (Passage D):

> The red-gold spools of their hands and their faces swinging
> Hither and thither across the high crystalline frame
> Of day:

with Thomas Hardy's 'Throwing a Tree' (Passage B):

> The two executioners stalk along over the knolls,
> Bearing two axes with heavy heads shining and wide

Hardy's stark 'executioners' which 'stalk' almost monosyllabically 'over the knolls' present a much more menacing and sinister picture than Lawrence's gentler, rhythmic 'hither and thither' image of men at work. The underlying difference is that Hardy is angry and sad about the destruction of the tree. Lawrence is simply marvelling at the beauty and dignity of the 'red-gold spools of their hands' as the road-gang moves. Both poets, however, focus on the early morning light – with different effects. Lawrence's 'high crystalline frame/ Of day' evokes a sense of wonder. For Hardy the light merely stresses the purpose of the 'heavy' 'shining and wide' axes.

Personal Writing

>> Task 6.7

1. Write a detailed and accurate, but imaginative, description of people you have seen at (any kind of) work.

2. Write a story set in an unusual workplace – perhaps a space station, a mortuary or a submarine?

3. Write a poem about people at work doing something which fascinates or angers you.

4. Describe your own working day as if you were working for a weekend newspaper. Make it a witty account if you wish.

5. Interview someone about his or her work and write it up as if you were a 21st century Mayhew.

6. Write about work in any way you wish.

Writing tip

When you want to write a poem start by jotting down phrases at random – perhaps a couple of adjectives and a noun ('long limp two-handled saw' or 'ringing cerulean mining').

When you have a number of these you can start to organise them into a poetic shape.

Don't forget – although you might decide you want it to – poetry doesn't have to rhyme. Neither does it necessarily need a regular rhythm. All words, phrases and so on have a rhythm of their own and for some poets that is enough.

Be prepared to work on your poem for some time and to keep revisiting your work until you're happy with it. The poet Charles Causley (1917-2003) once said in an interview that he redrafted every poem at least 25 times!

WORD BANK

Words such as **rick**, **speech** and **wheel** (used by Thomas Hardy in Passage A) are derived from the language which was spoken in Britain before the arrival in England of the Normans in 1066. Rick comes from *hreac*, speech from *specan* and wheel from *hweol*. This language is known as Old English and you will see it referred to in dictionaries as OE. Experts now regard it as rather inaccurate and misleading to call it Anglo-Saxon as it used to be known.

After 1066 OE merged gradually with Norman French, through which we gained most of our Latin-derived words – to form Middle English, the language used by Chaucer in 'The Canterbury Tales'. Eventually this evolved into Modern English as used by Shakespeare and ever since.

We get most of our short, everyday words such as **and**, **the**, **but**, **walk**, **sit**, **yes** – and so on – from OE. Words with gn (gnome, gnat) kn (knee, knife) or gh (high, eight) come from it too.

This is partly why English is such a rich language. Often OE already had a word. Then it acquired a synonym – sometimes several – from French and Latin. Thus we absorbed **beer** from French to add to the existing word **ale** and **serviette** to sit alongside OE's **napkin** – and there are hundreds of other examples.

›› Task 6.8

Pair up these OE words with their Latin-derived synonyms. Then use all 16 words in sentences of your own.

drink	consume
truthful	acrimonious
happiness	imbibe
hunger	felicity
bitter	veracious
eat	voracity
shortage	paucity
enough	sufficient

>> Task 6.9

Work with a partner. Test each other on these spellings – all words taken from the passages in this chapter – until you are both sure of them.

1. palette
2. altogether
3. cupboard
4. anxious
5. crystalline

6. luxuriant
7. foresight
8. achieves
9. economical
10. gossiping

Gerunds and gerundives
The -ing form of a verb is often 'borrowed' for adjectival use. For example:

the **penetrating** hum of the thresher
gossiping remarks
the **living** mast
the **blazing** sun

An -ing word used in this way is known as a **gerundive** (think of adjec<u>tive</u> and gerund<u>ive</u>).

Verb forms ending in -ing can also be used as nouns. For example:

to their **thinking**
increased to a **raving**
singing is my favourite leisure activity
he hates **swimming**

Sometimes called 'verbal nouns' these are more formally known as **gerunds**.

So, to sum up: gerundives behave like adjectives and gerunds act like nouns. Both end in -ing.

>> Task 6.10

Write two sentences for each of these words. Use it as a gerundive in the first and a gerund in the second. Write which it is in brackets.

For example: writing

> When I was in Year 2 we had a wonderful teacher whose speciality was writing lessons. (gerundive)

> Reading, writing and 'rithmetic are sometimes, rather inaccurately, called the three Rs. (gerund)

1. coughing
2. running
3. counting
4. dreaming

5. swinging
6. circling
7. typing
8. mending

>> Task 6.11

Make up eight sentences each using an -ing word as either a gerund or a gerundive. Write in brackets after each sentence which it is as you did in Task 6.10.

Effect and affect

Make sure you understand the difference between **effect** and **affect**.

When we write about literature and other texts, we often mention the effect of a word or comment on its effectiveness. **Effect** is (usually) a noun meaning **something caused** or **a result** or **influence**.

Thus we say: 'I like the effect of the light shining on your dress'.

Or we can turn it into an adjective and say: 'The light shining on your dress is effective.'

Affect, on the other hand, is almost always a verb meaning to make a difference. 'Does this train cancellation affect your journey?' Or 'Is he affected by the wet weather?'

If it helps learn the sentence: Smoking **a**ffects my **a**sthma.

Laying and lying

To lie is a verb. It means either **to put oneself in a horizontal position** or **to tell untruths**.

The past tense for the first meaning is **lay** (I lay on the grass all day yesterday) or **have lain** (I have lain on the grass all morning and now it's time for lunch).

At weekends (if you're lucky) you might enjoy a lie-in – and it is an error to call it anything else.

The untruth sense is easier. The past tense is lied or have lied. For example: 'I lied to him yesterday because I have always lied to him.'

The verb to lay is used when the person carrying out the action (the verb's subject) is doing something to something else (in other words when the the verb is being used transitively). So you can lay eggs (if you happen to be a hen), bricks, carpets or tables. The past tense is laid or have laid, as in new-laid eggs or a well-laid table.

Remember we're dealing with three different verbs here. Try not to muddle them.

Note: American English has different rules about laying and lying, so you may see what appear to be mistakes – but are not – in some books.

>> Task 6.12

Make up six sentences using effect and affect (or a form of them) correctly and six sentences using lay, lie, laid, lain, lied, laying, lying in as many correct combinations as you can.

More speaking and listening activities

> Collect poems and prose extracts about different aspects of work. Organise a session during which class members read them aloud.

> Prepare a polished performance for the class (or for an assembly?) of one of the passages in this chapter.

> Discuss the following question in a small group: 'Should we work to live or live to work?'

> Listen to an audio recording of *Tess of the D'Urbervilles* such as the 1997 Naxos recording read by Imogen Stubbs. Or watch the 1978 film *Tess* directed by Roman Polanski or the 1998 film *Tess of the D'Urbervilles* starring Justine Waddell. Tell someone else in the class what you thought of it and why. You will get more out of this activity if you read Hardy's novel first!

JUST FOR FUN

I play this very simple word game in my head while I'm having treatment at the dentist and need something to focus my mind on. I think that proves you can do it anywhere! Try it on your own or with a partner.

Think of a novelist for every letter of the alphabet (Austen, Brontë, Conrad …)
Or a poet (Auden, Browning, Coleridge …)
Or a book title (*Anne of Green Gables, Black Beauty, Charlotte's Web* …)

You can, of course do this with anything you choose: adverbs of movement (actively, briskly, cautiously …), capital cities (Ankara, Berlin, Canberra …), birds (albatross, bluetit, crow …).

WIDE RANGE READING

Far from the Madding Crowd by Thomas Hardy (1874) is the story of young Bathsheba Everdene who has inherited a farm and is trying to run it. She has three suitors, one of whom, Gabriel Oak, is a shepherd. As well as being an enjoyable read, the novel includes a lot of background about the work of shepherds and – as in *Tess of the D'Urbervilles* – everyday life in 19th century farming. The scene in which Oak's sheep get a bloating illness and the one in which the workers gather to celebrate having brought in the harvest are especially memorable.

The Great Stink by Clare Clark (2005). Set in 1855 this novel is about sewer workers and the building of new sewers under London. It is an exciting (if smelly!) read with a fascinating background to a tale of murder and corruption. Clark places Henry Mayhew's *London Labour and the London Poor* first in her list of sources. Novels which feature Victorian sewers seem to be quite fashionable. Try *Sweet Thames* by Matthew Kneale (1992) or *Montmorency* by Eleanor Updale (2003) for example, too.

The Lady and the Unicorn (2003) and *Burning Bright* (2007) both by Tracy Chevalier. *The Lady and the Unicorn* is about 15th century Belgian tapestry weavers and – in the same spirit as *Girl with a Pearl Earring* – a well-known tapestry now in France. Chevalier's *Burning Bright* features the poet, artist and free-thinker William Blake (1757-1827). Readers learn a lot about how he might have worked.

Dombey and Son by Charles Dickens (1848) tells the story of a businessman and his family – especially his (mostly) unhappy children. Read it for the usual colourful Dickensian tale, but also for the picture it gives of Victorian office and business life. There are also wonderful passages about the building and use of the railways which, in 1848, were just beginning to come into their own as a means of transport.

I Found my Horn by Jasper Rees (2008). The author of this rather original book is, like Mayhew, a journalist. As a journalistic project Rees set himself the task of re-learning the French horn in a single year – 22 years after he left school and gave it up. His 'horn year' was spent not only practising the instrument, but in investigating its history and interviewing horn players all over Europe and the USA. At the end he meets the challenge he has set himself and plays part of a Mozart concerto in public. As well as being an interesting book *I Found my Horn* shows you how a 21st century journalist works.

The Mozart Question by Michael Morpurgo (2007). This short novel – really a long short story – also has a journalist as its main narrator and is also musical in flavour. She goes to Venice to interview a world-famous violinist and hears an astonishing story about his parents, both violinists and both concentration camp survivors. This is very easy to read and there are lovely illustrations by Michael Foreman.

The Morning Gift by Eva Ibbotson (1993) is another novel written for teenagers. It opens in Vienna and is about the part-Jewish daughter of a university teacher who has to leave the country when the Nazis annexe Austria at the beginning of World War Two. But she needs help to get away and it comes from Quin, a London university professor and associate of her father. What follows is a delightful tale of misunderstandings and twists set mostly in London where Ruth, eventually, becomes a student. The background on Quin's work as a palaeontologist and Ruth's as a student in the 1940s is very well done.

Hamlet by William Shakespeare (1601) – Gravediggers – Act 5, scene 1. Hamlet, Prince of Denmark, has been sent away to England for several months and returns later in this scene. During his absence his beloved Ophelia has drowned, although he doesn't know that until he stumbles upon two men cheerfully digging her grave. The scene begins as a short, relatively light moment in a long tragic play. It also gives insights into the gravediggers' work and their attitude to it. In some older editions of the play they are called 'clowns' rather than gravediggers because their job in the play is to make jokes and they are not noblemen.

MOVING ON

- **Find out, if you don't know, who the Tolpuddle Martyrs were and why they were important.**

- **Look at some reproductions of paintings by Vermeer – perhaps in an art book – and then reread Passage E and/or the whole of *Girl with a Pearl Earring*. How many of the objects and furnishings Chevalier describes can you spot?**

- **Read Henry Mayhew's *London Labour and the London Poor*. Then use the internet to find out about the 21st century poor in cities such as Calcutta. Do you notice any similarities?**

READY FOR A REAL CHALLENGE?

Build your own anthology of poems about work in some of its many different forms. Comb books of poetry to find them. Experiment with writing a detailed analysis of one or two of your favourites, perhaps comparing one with another.

A Passage to India 7

What does the word 'India' make you think of? Gruelling street and rural poverty? Beautiful buildings? Tea plantations? Bollywood films? Spicy food? The Hindu religion? State-of-the-art modern computer technology? The truth is India is all these things and many more.

A British colony until 1947, India has inspired two sorts of literature. First, there is a lot of writing by British people looking at life in India from an outside point of view, mostly during the Colonial Period – often known as the British Raj. The extract from *The Jewel in the Crown* (Passage C) is, for example, really about ex-patriot Britons and their way of life. So is Kipling's poem (Passage D). Second, there is now a large body of literature written in English by Indians about India and Indian experience. Poems and novels show the life and thinking of Indian people from the inside. The Rohinton Mistry extract (Passage B) falls into this category. Passage A is different again because it is a piece of travel journalism describing the pleasures of north India for a tourist to visit.

The title of this chapter comes from a poem by the American poet Walt Whitman (1819–1892). EM Forster used it for the title of his 1924 novel which was made into an award-winning film directed by David Lean in 1984. It tells the story of a young English woman who alleges that she has been attacked by an Indian in a cave.

Passage A

1 Most newspapers have a regular section in which journalists write about places they have visited and to which readers might like
5 to travel. Often, though, that is all the readers will do - read. They will never actually visit the place described.
Journalists call them 'armchair travellers'.
10 So in some ways travel journalism has a similar function to fiction. It aims to interest and entertain the reader by conveying a strong sense of place with plenty of colours,
15 sounds, smells and tastes. The style, however, is usually rather different from most fiction as this piece about North
20 India, close to the Tibetan border, shows.

Everywhere, I see dark-eyed boys selling the softest multi-coloured, embroidered and sequined, paisley shawls in the late afternoon sun. The shawls hang outside the stalls that tumble onto the streets of McLeod Ganj, high in the Dhauladhar range of the Himalayas, northern India. Their brilliant splashes of colour clash gorgeously with the burgundy robes of the monks who walk through the streets, mobile phones clasped to their shaven heads – the town is home to the Dalai Lama, who was granted official asylum in India after fleeing Tibet in 1959.

Tibet is everywhere: Buddhist prayers swirl through the air and lines of coloured Tibetan prayer flags, some faded, some bright primary blue, yellow and red, are strung through trees and across streets. They

A street in McLeod Ganj

25   flutter in the warm mountain breeze, but the sun dazzles on the snowy mountain peaks, which provide an almost cinematic backdrop to McLeod Ganj.

    The town, encompassing Lower Dharamsala, was named after the governor of the Punjab, David McLeod, who established it as a British garrison in the 1850s. This British link aside, the town is otherwise defined by Buddhism. Well-shod, middle-aged travellers in wide-brimmed hats with expensive bags and good cameras are in 30   evidence, as this is an epicentre for anyone interested in Tibetan politics and culture. Richard Gere has been spotted here, and locals still murmur about the day Cindy Crawford sashayed between the beggars to buy shawls.

    But it's also a magnet for a certain type of late-teenage gap-year traveller. Dreadlocked, sunburnt and travel weary, they write postcards home and flirt 35   unashamedly over plates of dhal and bottles of icy Kingfisher beer – the King of Good Times – in the local restaurants. So as well as holiness, the town sizzles with another sort of energy from the backpackers, staying in the Mountain Cloud Hostel, drinking at Jimmy's Bar or going for an Ayurvedic massage at the Home Indian Massage Room.

40   This fusion of the holy and something more carnal creates a surprisingly enlightened atmosphere; although the town is full of tourists, it doesn't feel spoiled or over-sold. Monks, teenagers, shawl-sellers and rickshaw drivers inhabit the town with jolly and companionable ease. Stacked up like Lego, the Buddhist monastic complex was built – and continues to grow – in a haphazard way.

45   The hot stink of His Holiness's Holy Cows hits you as you circumnavigate the hill on the Holy Walk. Little shrines dot the path, cluttered with flags and carved prayer stones, and oddly incongruous little objects of spiritual significance. Crows the size of dogs peck at piles of tsampa, barley meal mixed with butter, which the monks eat for breakfast. In the Kalachakra Chapel, the walls are decorated with winking gods and

50   fabulous coloured animals, like a kitsch, Eastern-version of the Sistine Chapel.

By Clover Stroud, www.telegraph.co.uk, 7th January 2008

>> Task 7.1

1. Suggest a heading for this passage. Remember that it has to summarise the content of the piece and to attract the reader's attention. Journalists call such a heading a 'catch-line' because its job is to catch the reader.

2. Summarise in your own words – incorporating short quotations (using inverted commas) from the passage – the contrasts in McLeod Ganj which surprised the writer.

3. Clover Stroud uses the present tense and addresses her reader directly. Why do you think she does this and how well does it work in your view?

4. Comment in detail on these comparisons: (a) an epicentre (line 30), (b) stacked up like Lego (line 43), and (c) crows the size of dogs (line 47). Before you write it might help you do discuss with a partner:

   • how well you think they work

   • what you associate with whatever the thing depicted is being compared to – epicentre, dogs, Lego (formally such an association is known as a connotation)

   • why they are or are not appropriate

   • whether or not you like their originality.

Passage B

1

Rohinton Mistry was born in Bombay (usually now referred to as Mumbai) in India in 1952 but has lived in Canada since

5 he was 23. His powerful novel A Fine Balance is a story about four people whose lives overlap in the city in the mid-

10 1970s when India is a troubled country because prime minister Indira Gandhi has just defied a court order to resign, declared a state of emergency and put her opponents in prison. It is a long book with

15 lots of eccentric minor characters and a strong storyline - a bit like Dickens set in 20th century India. Terrible misfortunes befall some of Mistry's characters but it's

20 a very positive book and, at the end, spirits are still high. In this passage one of the characters in difficulty turns to the local

25 market for solace.

He found the jyotshis and fortune-tellers in the marketplace most comforting. They offered solutions to his money problems, and advice on improving his future, which was becoming his past at an alarming velocity. He discovered their confident pronouncements to be a soothing drug.

Nor did he restrict himself to palmists and astrologers. Seeking stronger drugs, he turned to less orthodox messengers: card-picking doves, chart-reading parrots, communicating cows, diagram-divining snakes. Always worried that an acquaintance would spot him during one of his questionable excursions, he decided, with great reluctance, to leave behind his distinctive fez. It was like abandoning a dear friend. The only time he had forsaken this fixture of daily wear was during

Partition, back in 1947, when communal slaughter at the brand new border had ignited riots everywhere. In certain areas it was wisest to go bareheaded, for choosing

30 incorrectly from among fez, white cap, and turban could mean losing one's head.

Fortunately his sittings at the avian auguries were relatively private. He could crouch unnoticed on a pavement corner with the creature's keeper, ask the question, and the dove or parrot would hop out of its cage to enlighten him.

The cow session, on the other hand, was a major performance that collected large

35 crowds. The cow, caparisoned in colourful brocaded fabrics, a string of tiny bells round her neck, was led into the ring of spectators by a man with a drum. Though the fellow's shirt and turban were bright-hued, he seemed quite drab compared to the richly bedizened cow. The two walked the circle: once, twice, thrice – however long it took him to recite the cow's curriculum vitae, with special emphasis on prophecies and

40 forecasts accurately completed to date. His voice was deafeningly raucous, his eyes

bloodshot, his gestures manic, and all this frenzy was calculated as a masterly counterpoint to the cow's calm demeanour. After the brief biography was narrated, the drum that had silently hung from his shoulder came to life. It was a drum meant not for beating but for rubbing. He continued to walk the cow in a circle, rubbing the drumskin
45 with a stick, producing a horrible bleating, a groaning, a wailing. It was a sound to wake the dead and stun the living, it was eldritch, it was a summons to spirits and forces not of this world, a summons to descend, witness, and assist bovine divination.

When the drum ceased, the man shouted the paying customer's questions into the cow's ear, loud enough for the entire ring of humans to hear. And she answered with
50 a nod or a shake of her intricately made-up head, tinkling her tiny silver bells round her neck. The crowd applauded in wonder and admiration. Then the drum-rubbing resumed while donations were collected.

One day, after Ibrahim's question was bellowed into the soft, brown, unprotected ear, there was no response. The man repeated it louder. This time the cow reacted.
55 Whether it was the annoying drum that she had put up with for years, or the boorish bellowing in her ear day after day, she gored her keeper with her vermilioned horns.

For a moment, the spectators thought the cow was just responding a bit more energetically than usual to the question. Then she tossed him to the ground, trampling him thoroughly. Now they realised it was not part of the prophecy
60 procedure, especially when the man's blood started to flow.

From *A Fine Balance* by Rohinton Mistry (1995)

>> Task 7.2

1. Summarise what you learn from this passage about the market place and the people who work in it.

2. How does the cow's owner create an atmosphere of mystery? Answer in as much detail as you can and include short quotations from the passage in your answer.

3. What can you deduce from this passage about the author's attitude to the fortune telling in the market? Take evidence from the passage to support your answer.

4. What does this passage have in common with Passage A? In what ways is it different? Discuss this with a partner and then write your answer in as much detail as you can. Consider the:

   - place being described
   - people in the passage and how the author tells you about them
   - way the two authors use language – particularly adjectives and verbs
   - authors' attitude and how much you are aware of him or her in the passage.

Passage C

The Jewel in the Crown is set amidst growing anti-British feeling in India in the early 1940s. Daphne Manners is attacked in the Bibighar Gardens. Attempts, some of them very misguided, by the British authorities to find and punish the attacker lead to racism, hatred and brutality being heaped on Daphne's Indian lover who is not, of course the culprit. In a way these 'small' events are a reflection of what is happening across the country as more and more Indians decide they want home rule as this extract explains. Miss Crane is a fairly typical ex-patriot. Mahatma Gandhi, prime minister of India, was shot by an assassin in 1948. The title of this novel, by the way, is a quotation from Queen Victoria who called India the 'jewel in the crown' because she regarded it as the best bit of her empire.

In 1942, which was the year the Japanese defeated the British army in Burma and Mr Gandhi began preaching sedition in India the English, then living in the civil and military cantonment of Mayapore, had to admit that the future did not look propitious. They had faced bad times before, though, and felt that they could face them again, that now they knew where they stood and there could be no more heart-searching for quite a while yet about the rights and wrongs of their colonial-imperialist policy and administration.

As they were fond of putting it at the club, it was a question of first things first, and when they heard that Miss Crane, the supervisor of the district's Protestant mission schools, had taken Mr Gandhi's picture down from the walls of her study and no longer entertained Indian ladies to tea but English soldiers instead, they were grateful to her as well as amused. In peace time opinions could be as diverse and cranky as you wished. In war you had to close the ranks; and if it was to be a question of sides Miss Crane seemed to have shown at last which she was really on.

What few people knew was that the Indian ladies themselves had taken the initiative over the question of tea on Tuesdays at Edwina Crane's bungalow. Miss Crane suspected that it was the ladies' husbands who had dissuaded them from making the weekly appearance, not only because Mr Gandhi's picture had gone but in such cases visits could have been thought of, in this explosive year, as buttering-up of the raj. What hurt her most was that none of the ladies had bothered to discuss their reasons with her. They had one by one or two by two just stopped coming and made feeble excuses when she met any of them in the bazaar or on her way to the mission school-rooms.

Mahatma Gandhi leading an anti-Empire demonstration, 1930

She was sorry about the ladies whom she had always encouraged to be frank with her, but not at all sorry about Mr Gandhi's portrait. The ladies had an excuse. Mr Gandhi did not. She believed he was behaving abominably. She felt, in fact, let down. For years she had laughed at the Europeans who said that he was not to be trusted, but now Mr Gandhi had extended what looked like an open invitation to the Japanese to come and help him rid India of the British – and if he thought they would be the better masters then she could only assume he was out of his senses or, which was worse, revealing that his philosophy of non-violence had a dark side that added up to total invalidation of its every aspect. The Japanese were, apparently, to do his violence for him.

Reacting from her newly found mistrust of the Mahatma and her disappointment in the behaviour of the ladies (the kind of disappointment she had actually become no stranger to) she wondered whether her life might not have been better spent among her own people, persuading them to appreciate the qualities of Indians, instead of among Indians attempting to prove that at least one Englishwoman admired and respected them.

From *The Jewel in the Crown*, the first part of The Raj Quartet, by Paul Scott (1966)

>> Task 7.3

1. Summarise what you learn about Miss Crane from this passage. Include:

    *   her job
    *   her beliefs
    *   her behaviour.

2. We do not hear Miss Crane's voice directly in this passage. It is written entirely in reported indirect speech.

    a. Do you think this works?

    b. Would it have been more effective if Paul Scott had given us some of Miss Crane's conversation in full?

    c. How else would it have changed the style and tone of the passage if he had?

3. This passage mentions yet another Indian market place – the bazaar. What impression do you get of this one? Why do you think it is not described in the detail that the writers of Passages A and B used?

Passage D

Rudyard Kipling was born in Bombay (Mumbai) in 1865 to British parents. He was sent to Britain from age six to go to school. He worked in India as a journalist between 1882 and 1889. Some of his best-known work comes from those years and was first published in newspapers. In this poem he is marvelling at the difference in atmosphere between trying to celebrate Christmas in an exotic, hot country and how it might be back in Britain. Look carefully at his descriptions of the sights, smells and sounds of India. Tamarisks, by the way, are trees which need a warmish climate. They grow in Asia and the Mediterranean.

Christmas in India

1 Dim dawn behind the tamarisks—the sky is saffron-yellow—
      As the women in the village grind the corn,
  And the parrots seek the riverside, each calling to his fellow
      That the Day, the staring Easter Day, is born.
5   Oh the white dust on the highway! Oh the stenches in the byway!

Oh the clammy fog that hovers over earth!
And at Home they're making merry 'neath the white and scarlet berry—
What part have India's exiles in their mirth?

Full day behind the tamarisks—the sky is blue and staring—
10　　As the cattle crawl afield beneath the yoke,
And they bear One o'er the field-path, who is past all hope or caring,
To the ghat below the curling wreaths of smoke.
Call on Rama, going slowly, as ye bear a brother lowly—
Call on Rama—he may hear, perhaps, your voice!
15　　With our hymn-books and our psalters we appeal to other altars,
And to-day we bid 'good Christian men rejoice!'

High noon behind the tamarisks—the sun is hot above us—
As at Home the Christmas Day is breaking wan.
They will drink our healths at dinner—those who tell us how they love us,
20　　And forget us till another year be gone!
Oh the toil that knows no breaking! Oh the Heimweh, ceaseless, aching!
Oh the black dividing Sea and alien Plain!
Youth was cheap—wherefore we sold it. Gold was good—we hoped to hold it,
And to-day we know the fulness of our gain.

25　Grey dusk behind the tamarisks—the parrots fly together—
As the sun is sinking slowly over Home;
And his last ray seems to mock us shackled in a lifelong tether.
That drags us back how'er so far we roam.
Hard her service, poor her payment—she in ancient, tattered raiment—
30　　India, she the grim Stepmother of our kind.
If a year of life be lent her, if her temple's shrine we enter,
The door is shut—we may not look behind.

Black night behind the tamarisks—the owls begin their chorus—
As the conches from the temple scream and bray.
35　With the fruitless years behind us, and the hopeless years before us,
Let us honour, O my brother, Christmas Day!
Call a truce, then, to our labours—let us feast with friends and neighbours,
And be merry as the custom of our caste;
For if 'faint and forced the laughter', and if sadness follow after,
40　　We are richer by one mocking Christmas past.

'Christmas in India' by Rudyard Kipling (1886)

>> Task 7.4

1. How does what the narrator sees around him contrast with what he imagines will be happening in England at the same time?

2. What is the mood of the poem?

   - Look closely at the words Kipling chooses such as **toil, shackled, stenches** and **hopeless**.

   - It might help you to discuss this with a partner before you answer in writing.

   - Try making a list of words which strike you both as interesting or significant.

   - You might find the words **negative** and **positive** useful.

3a. What does the narrator mean by 'Hard her service, poor her payment—she in ancient, tattered raiment—/ India, she the grim Stepmother of our kind?'

  b. What do you learn from these two lines about the narrator's feelings?

4. Look at Kipling's use of rhyme both at the ends of lines and within them. Write about the rhythm this creates. What do you think it adds to the poem?

Writing about literature

Study this example of how a sentence of travel writing (taken from Passage A) can be commented on in detail.

> Tibet is everywhere: Buddhist prayers swirl through the air and lines of coloured Tibetan prayer flags, some faded, some bright primary blue, yellow and red, are strung through trees and across streets.

The first three words in this sentence make a clear statement. The rest – pivoted on the colon – amplifies the initial declaration. It is as if the writer is providing evidence in support of her observation. Her very visual description relies heavily on colour ('primary blue', 'yellow' and 'red') and on strong verbs of movement such as 'swirl' and 'strung'. It is however an interesting mixture of literal and metaphorical description. The prayers 'swirl' only metaphorically, whereas the prayer flags are literally 'strung through trees and across streets'. The use of two proper adjectives 'Buddhist' and 'Tibetan' ensure that this is convincing as an accurate, carefully placed description as well as a colourful, imaginative account.

>> Task 7.5

Choose a sentence from Passage A and comment on it in as much detail as you can.

Personal Writing

>> Task 7.6

1. Write a vivid and colourful account of a place you have visited in Britain or abroad as if you were a travel journalist. It doesn't have to be very far away or very exotic – as long as you can make it seem exciting and attractive. (I once wrote, and had published in a newspaper, an article about the Isle of Sheppey in Kent which is very close to my home and not really a holiday destination, for example.) Try to use original comparisons as Clover Stroud does.

2. Read one of the books featuring India in the 'Wide Range Reading' section of this chapter and write a review of it for the school magazine.

3. Talk to a partner about (or discuss in a small group) your feelings about one country taking over another and making it into a colony. Anything you have read here or elsewhere about the Raj might help you, but bring in any other examples you want to. Then write your views in an essay. Plan it point by point before you start and make sure you begin with an introduction and end with a conclusion.

4. Write a story or a poem about (or narrated by) someone who is a long way from home.

5. Write a continuation of the story which is being told in Passage B or Passage C.

6. Write about India in any way you wish.

Writing tip

When you are writing journalistically about places, focus on the detail of what you can see, hear, smell, taste and feel. Concentrate on a few vivid details rather than trying to describe the whole of a place in general terms. So devote a sentence or two to one mewing, scavenging, red-beaked seagull you see in the street rather than say there were masses of gulls. Write about the sugary, sweaty smell of fried onions tainting (perfuming?) your hair, clothes, mouth and nose rather than say there are several burger bars. Your aim is to bring the place alive for someone who has never been there.

 WORD BANK

The word **kitsch** which Clover Stroud uses in Passage A is an adjective meaning **vulgar**, **tawdry** or **pretentious**. It came into English from German during the 20th century.

Words have entered English from many other languages. There are two main reasons for this.

Often English speakers simply adopted a word from somewhere else because they didn't have a word of their own which expressed that particular idea – **kitsch** is one of these. So is **cul-de-sac** from French and **graffiti** from Italian. It is a two-way process. French, for example, has taken words like *le parking* and *le weekend* from English.

The other main reason is that from the 16th to the 19th centuries Britain colonised many countries across the world. The English language picked up words from the countries it occupied, such as **bungalow** from India, **totem** from Africa and **kangaroo** (no prizes for guessing where this last one comes from!).

➤➤ Task 7.7

Look up these everyday English words in a good dictionary. Find out where each came from and make a brief note on the origin of each.

1.	tempo	7.	pyjamas
2.	restaurant	8.	potato
3	tofu	9.	anorak
4.	blitz	10.	poncho
5.	safari	11.	ballet
6.	paparazzi	12.	burkha

Rohinton Mistry's word **vermilioned** means **reddened** or **painted red**. The word **vermilion** – red – comes form the Latin word *vermis*, a worm, because it was originally a pigment made from worms' bodies. (Vermicelli is pasta shaped like little worms, vermiform means worm-shaped and the word vermin is, of course, related.)

English is rich in colour words to suggest different shades and moods. All these adjectives, for example, mean red: crimson, rufous, coral, maroon, cerise, cardinal, scarlet, carmine, rosy.

These words all suggest shades of blue: cobalt, azure, sapphire, indigo, navy, cerulean.

➤➤ Task 7.8

1. List as many words as you can think of or find (a good Thesaurus could help) which mean (a) green and (b) yellow. Stick, as in the examples above, to one-word adjectives which do not need the name of the colour as well to make their meaning clear. So just as the examples left out brick red and sky blue, ignore Lincoln green and sunshine yellow.

   _____

2. Write three sentences each using a different word which means white.

   _____

3. Write three sentences each using a different word which means black.

>> Task 7.9

Use each of the following words in a sentence of your own to show and practise your understanding of its meaning. All are taken from this chapter's passages. When you have finished check that you know the spelling of each, perhaps by working with a partner and testing each other.

1. asylum
2. sequined
3. incongruous
4. pronouncements
5. propitious

6. prophecies
7. psalters
8. dissuaded
9. companionable
10. invalidation

 NUTS AND BOLTS

An overview of the different ways in which sentences can be organised can help you to write with more confidence and accuracy.

Study this sentence:

The town, encompassing Lower Dharamsala, was named after the governor of the Punjab, David McLeod, who established it as a British garrison in the 1850s.

At its heart is one central statement known as a main clause. If it were used as a sentence on its own it would still make sense:

The town, encompassing Lower Dharamsala, **was named after the governor of the Punjab**, David McLeod, who established it as a British garrison in the 1850s.

'The town was named after the governor of the Punjab.' summarises the long sentence.

The full sentence gives three other pieces of information:

The town, (1) **encompassing Lower Dharamsala**, was named after the governor of the Punjab, (2) **David McLeod**, (3) **who established it as a British garrison in the 1850s**.

- 'encompassing Lower Dharamsala' is an adjectival phrase which qualifies the word 'town' by telling you more about it. Because is it an adjectival phrase which interrupts the main clause it is marked off with a pair of commas.

- 'David McLeod' is a phrase in apposition. That means it is grammatically parallel to something else – in this case it is a proper noun lying alongside – in apposition to – the noun phrase 'the governor of the Punjab'. It is another way of referring to the governor. This phrase is marked off with a pair of commas too.

- 'who established it as a British garrison in the 1850s' is a clause (not a phrase) because it has a verb of its own – 'established'. It works like an adjective qualifying David McLeod by giving you more information about him. It is therefore known as an adjectival clause. The writer could have chosen to put this information in a separate simple sentence – 'He established it as a British garrison in the 1850s'. Instead she chose to knit four ideas together into a **complex** sentence.

Phrases and clauses which add extra information to a sentence's main clause are know as **subordinate** (phrases and clauses). Alternatively they are sometimes called dependent phrases and clauses because they are 'hung' on the sentence (from the Latin *pendere* to hang – think of pendant and pendulum).

›› Task 7.10

Write these sentences and in each case underline the main clause. Then write it as if it were a free-standing sentence or summary of the whole. You will need to adjust the punctuation.

1. Back at Gemma's house, I went into the sitting room which was very large and untidy.

2. I wondered, as I looked around me, who had built the cathedral which towered above us.

3. Our neighbour, Elsie Smith, whom we try to help as much as we can, is very elderly.

4. Carrots, when they are braised, peas, freshly shelled, and broccoli which has been cooked in cheese sauce, are my favourite vegetables.

5. Jess, my cousin, usually goes swimming with Louisa who lives near her.

6. Wondering whom she should contact first, my mother phoned Ben's parents when he fell from our tree.

Writers often create longer sentences by constructing a series of equally important main clauses linked by a conjunction such as 'and', 'but' or 'for'. These are called **compound** sentences. For example:

> They had one by one or two by two just stopped coming and made feeble excuses when she met any of them in the bazaar or on her way to the mission school-rooms.

This is three separate statements (1) They had one by one or two by two just stopped coming (2) and made feeble excuses when she met any of them in the bazaar (3) or on her way to the mission school-rooms.

The writer could have written:

> They had one by one or two by two just stopped coming. They made feeble excuses when she met any of them in the bazaar. They also made excuses when she met them on her way to the mission school-rooms.

Splitting it into three sentences, however, makes it jerky and repetitive. Paul Scott's version is much better.

Good writers usually vary the length and shape of their sentences – some simple and short interspersed with longer compound and complex sentences.

>> Task 7.11

1. Create five complex sentences of your own. Start with a main clause, and then add some subordinate phrases and clauses. Be sure that each finished sentence begins with a capital letter and ends with a full stop and that you mark off subordinate phrases and clauses with commas unless they come at the end of the sentence.

---

2. Create three compound sentences in which statements of equal weight are linked with conjunctions.

NUTS AND BOLTS Most sentences include a subject. It may be one word such as 'I' or 'Maisie'. It may be something more complex such as 'Mr Opie, our popular and witty Year 9 English teacher…'.

As you know, the subject often comes at the beginning of the sentence, but it doesn't have to.

You also know that not far from the subject of any sentence is a verb – the action performed by the subject. The sentence may have other things too, but a subject and a verb are usually the basic building bricks.

It is important to make sure that your subject and verb agree. A singular subject needs a singular verb. If the subject is plural then, of course, it needs a plural verb.

This is obvious in sentences such as:

I danced.

Maisie deposited her bag on the table and shouted at the top of her voice.

Mr Opie, our popular and witty Year 9 English teacher, retires this year.

But be careful in sentences like this:

Peter and Evie are sister and brother. (Plural subject 'Peter and Evie' so not 'is')

The rain, the gloomy surroundings and the rotten accommodation were all responsible for our disappointing holiday. (Plural subject 'The rain, the gloomy surroundings and the rotten accommodation' so not 'was')

Everything is ready. (Singular subject 'everything' so not 'are')

Note that these words are all singular and need singular verbs to agree with them:

anybody	everybody	either
nobody	everyone	neither
anyone	everything	none
each		

For example:

> Neither of the women was available to comment. (not 'were')

> We lost several golf balls but none was found. (not 'were')

> Each of the ten spellings was harder than the one before. (not 'were')

Take care too with collective nouns, organisations and countries. They are singular:

> Save the Children, a large charity, is planning its next campaign. (not 'are')

> The band is waiting for its conductor. (not 'are')

> The flock of sheep munches grass almost continuously. (not 'munch')

>> Task 7.12

Write these sentences putting the correct form of an appropriate verb in the space.

1. 'Seventeen aircraft ... sent on a mission tonight but none ... lost,' announced the Second World War radio newsreader.

2. The lions ... nearly all day.

3. The pride of lions ... nearly all day.

4. North Korea ... asked for help from other countries.

5. Everybody ... a good meal.

6. Neither of the men ... found guilty at the end of the trial.

7. ... none of you ... of the Magna Carta?' demanded the exasperated history teacher.

8. Everyone in our class ... very distressed to hear the news.

9. The London Symphony Orchestra ... playing an all Beethoven concert at Bridgwater Hall tonight.

10. There are two ways of spelling judgement or judgment: either ... correct.

11. A splendid pack of timber wolves ... at Howletts, the conservation zoo in Kent.

12. Italy ... a longstanding member of the European Union.

Make sure that your subjects and verbs agree. Both must be singular or both must be plural. It is quite easy to make a mistake.

For example, these words are all singular. So they need singular verbs to agree with them:

anybody	everyone
everybody	everything
nobody	either
anyone	neither
each	none
	everybody

For example:

> **Neither** of the women **was** present. (not **were**).
>
> Six planes took off but **none has** yet landed. (not **have**)
>
> **Each** of the twenty quizzes **was** harder than the one before (not **were**).

Take care too with collective nouns such as a **pride** of lions or a **gang** of thieves. They are singular. So, not only do they need singular verbs, they also need singular possessives such as 'its' rather than 'their'. For example:

- The school **is** planning **its** next fundraising event. (not **are**).
- The band **is** waiting for **its** conductor (not **are**).
- The flock of sheep **eats** for most of the day (not **eat**).

Note: You can usually change sentences like these to make the subject plural without altering the meaning if you prefer:

- All the pupils and teachers in the school are planning their next fundraising event.
- Band players are waiting for their conductor.
- All the sheep in the flock eat for most of the day.

›› Task 7.13

Fill in the gaps in these sentences. Some have singular subjects and some plural.

1. All members of the orchestra … eagerly looking forward to playing Beethoven's Fifth Symphony.

2. The orchestra … eagerly looking forward to playing Beethoven's Fifth Symphony.

3. The pack of cards … on the table.

4. The class … the school rules.

>> Task 7.13 (cont.)

5. All the students ... the school rules.

6. Each girl ... a locker of ... own.

7. All the girls ... lockers of ... own.

8. The zoo's new baby elephant was born to a herd which ... at Howlett's in Kent.

9. We have heard two versions of this event but neither ... true.

10. Why ... the team so scruffily dressed?

11. Why ... team players so scruffily dressed?

12. Our local choir ... lost ... rehearsal space.

More speaking and listening activities

Organise a class showing of Richard Attenborough's 1982 film *Gandhi* which is available on DVD. Watch and listen very carefully and think about how the film is made and what it is trying to say. Then compare views with a partner about what you each found most interesting about the film.

Prepare a lively reading of Kipling's poem 'Christmas in India' (or choose another Kipling poem if you prefer. 'If' is his best known. 'Mandalay' and 'Danny Deever' are both worth studying too). Then perform it to the rest of the class or in an assembly.

Choose and research any aspect of India which interests you. Summarise what you have learned in a three-minute presentation for the rest of the class.

Organise a debate or a formal class discussion to consider whether or not Britain and other developed countries do enough to help the poor in India. If you opt for a proper debate you will need to decide on the wording of a proposition such as 'This house thinks that Britain does too little for the poor of India'. Either way, it is important that everyone taking part prepares carefully. You cannot reason or argue effectively without plenty of facts to support your points.

Numbers quiz

Try this numbers quiz. The answer to each clue is a book or play title with a number in it. For example:

Clue: Five – a Poirot story by Agatha Christie
Answer: *Five Little Pigs*

Clue: Nine – a novel by Michael Morpurgo
Answer: *The Nine Lives of Montezuma*

1. One – a novel by Eve Garnett

2. Two – a play by Shakespeare

3. Three – a novel by Alexander Dumas

4. Four – a novel by Andy McNab

5. Five – a novel by EE Nesbit

6. Six – a book of poems by AA Milne

7. Seven – the first title in a long series by Enid Blyton

8. Eight – a novel by Louisa M Alcott

9. Nine – one of Meg Cabot's *Princess Diaries*

10. Ten – a novel by Agatha Christie whose title had to be changed because the original, a line from a nursery rhyme, came to be regarded as offensive. But the ten stayed in!

WIDE RANGE READING

Staying On by Paul Scott (1977) is a sequel to the Raj Quartet. It is the story of Colonel 'Tusker' and Lucy Smalley who stay on in the hills of Pankot after India becomes independent. It won the Booker Prize, an important award, the year it was published. Scott died a year later.

The Far Pavilions by MM Kaye (1978) is a historical romance set in 19th century India in the foothills of the Himalayas. Like The Raj Quartet it was adapted into a very successful television series which you can now get on DVD.

Olivia and Jai by Rebecca Ryman (1990) is a love story set in the 1840s when it was not acceptable for a white American to fall in love with a man of mixed ancestry. There is, anyway, a mystery about him.

A Suitable Boy by Vikram Seth (1993), who has Indian ancestry and has lived in India as well as in Britain, the USA and China. *A Suitable Boy* tells the story of four families in India, after the Raj. At the centre of it all is an independently minded young Hindu woman whose family members are searching for 'a 'suitable boy' to be her husband. Don't be put off by the length. The story rolls along quite fast.

The God of Small Things by Arundhati Roy (1997) is another Booker Prize winner. This novel is about twins growing up in India. They have a loving mother and a nasty great aunt along with Uncle Chako whom they adore. This is a quirky story which shifts about in time and place but it is witty and pretty original.

The Inheritance of Loss by Kiran Desai (2006) was yet another Man Booker (it had a new name by 2006) Prize winner. It is the story of a crusty old judge living in what he would like to be retirement in the north-eastern Himalayas. Then his orphaned granddaughter Sai moves in and he is forced to rethink, especially when soldiers from Nepal become a threat and Sai has a romance blossoming with her tutor. The scenes when the judge is with his friends and neighbours are especially well done. This novel took the author eight years to write.

The Jungle Book by Rudyard Kipling (1894). Like Hardy and Lawrence, Kipling was an outstanding writer of prose as well as a poet. He wrote many stories and novels and once he had settled in Sussex was, for many years, Britain's most famous writer. *The Jungle Book* is a marvellous set of vivid, India-set short stories for children. Forget the Disney version and read the original Mowgli stories. Don't miss Riki-Tiki-Tavi either. It's a splendid story about a mongoose killing cobras in a garden and one of my all-time favourites.

Ganesh by Malcolm J Bosse (1984) is a moving and perceptive story for young adult readers about an orphaned Indian boy and how he copes – first with a funeral, then with grief and with everyday life.

Village by the Sea by Anita Desai (1982) has become something of a classic. Their mother is sick and their father is always drunk, so Lila and Hari are struggling to earn a family income and look after two younger sisters. Then Hari disappears to Bombay leaving Lila to cope alone. This is teenage fiction, but Anita Desai, who is half Indian and half German, has written many adult books set in India such as *Clear Light of Day* (1980). She is the mother of Kiran Desai – see above.

Ten Twentieth-Century Indian Poets edited by R Parthasarathy (1976). Oxford University Press has, for over 30 years, produced what is probably the best-known anthology of Indian poetry in English. There are notes on each poet and plenty of poems to read. It's a good way of sampling 'real' Indian English Literature and comparing it with British, American or other forms of English Literature.

MOVING ON

- Find out everything you can about the Dalai Lama and the history of his position.

- Watch the TV film *My Boy Jack* – available on DVD. Written by, and starring, actor David Haig who bears a startling resemblance to Rudyard Kipling, it tells the story of how Kipling's only son lost his life in the First World War. You also learn a lot about Kipling and his world. Film-makers used Batemans in Sussex, Kipling's house which now belongs to the National Trust, for the indoor family scenes. Daniel Radcliffe, of Harry Potter fame, plays Kipling's son, Jack.

- Make a large map of India – A3 size – for the classroom wall. Show rivers, towns, cities and as much other information as you can. Make sure you put on it every place and area mentioned in this chapter.

READY FOR A REAL CHALLENGE?

Make a short study of events in India during 1947 and 1948. Then consider what has happened there since. Can you find causes and connections?

What do we mean by old? Today nearly 10,000 people in Britain are aged 100 or more and centenarians are the fastest growing age group. Experts predict that by 2031 they will number 40,000. No wonder you can now buy 100th birthday cards easily in almost every card shop!

Until recently living to be over 100 would have been almost unheard of. When Shakespeare died in 1616, aged 56, he was regarded as an old man. Even a century ago 100th birthdays were very rare indeed. Now – because of good food and better hygiene and health care – you are quite likely to have fit and healthy grandparents or great grandparents in their 70s or 80s, or more, who play sport, travel and are very active.

Perhaps, as many older people will tell you, age is merely a state of mind, or 'just a number' as some people say. That was certainly true of Shakespeare's Cleopatra in his play *Antony and Cleopatra*. She was far from young but still so glamorously alluring that Antony couldn't resist her – with disastrous results. One of Antony's men says of Cleopatra that 'Age cannot wither her, nor custom stale/ her infinite variety'.

The passages in this chapter look at age from various points of view in fiction, poetry, a memoir, a play review and an obituary.

Passage A

1

Dickens again - and no apologies for offering you another sample of (probably)

5 *the greatest ever novelist in English. Here Pip, the narrator of Great Expectations, is taken, after work, to Wemmick's tiny home ('the castle') in the London suburbs.*

10 *Wemmick is assistant to Pip's lawyer, Jaggers, and quite different away from the office. He introduces Pip to his deaf old father.*

I expressed the readiness I felt, and we went into the castle. There we found, sitting by the fire, a very old man in a flannel coat: clean, cheerful, comfortable, and well cared for, but intensely deaf.

'Well Aged Parent', said Wemmick, 'and I wish you could hear his name. Nod away at him, Mr Pip; that's what he likes. Nod away at him, if you please, like winking!'

'This is a fine place of my

15 son's, sir', cried the old man, while I nodded as hard as I possibly could. 'This is a pretty pleasure-ground sir. This spot and these beautiful works upon it ought to be kept together by the Nation, after my son's time, for the people's enjoyment.'

'You're as proud of it as Punch, ain't you, Aged?' said Wemmick, contemplating the old man, with his hard face really softened. 'There's a nod for you', giving him a still more

20 tremendous one. 'You like that don't you? If you're not tired, Mr Pip – though I know it's tiring to strangers – will you tip him one more? You can't think how it pleases him.'

I tipped him several more, and he was in great spirits. We left him bestirring himself to feed the fowls, and we sat

25   down to our punch in the arbour where Wemmick told me as he smoked a pipe that it had taken him a good many years to bring the property up to its present pitch of perfection.

From the 1946 film of Great Expectations with Alec Guinness and John Mills

30   'Is it your own, Mr Wemmick?'

'O yes', said Wemmick, 'I have got hold of it, a bit at a time. It's a freehold, by George!'

'Is it indeed? I hope Mr Jaggers admires it?'

35   'Never seen it', said Wemmick. 'Never heard of it. Never seen the Aged. Never heard of him. No; the office is one thing, and private life is another. When I go into the office, I leave the Castle behind me. If it's not in any way disagreeable to you, you'll oblige me by doing the same. I don't wish it professionally spoken about.'

Of course I felt my good faith involved in the observance of his request. The punch
40   being very nice, we sat there drinking it and talking until almost nine o'clock. 'Getting near gun-fire', said Wemmick then, as he laid down his pipe, 'it's the Aged's treat.'

Proceeding into the Castle again, we found the Aged heating the poker, with expectant eyes, as a preliminary to the performance of this nightly ceremony. Wemmick stood with his watch in his hand, until the moment was come for him to
45   take the red-hot poker from the Aged, and repair to the battery. He took it, and went out, and presently the Stinger went off with a Bang that shook the crazy little box of a cottage as if it must fall to pieces, and made every glass and teacup ring. Upon this the Aged – who I believe would have been blown out of his arm-chair but for holding on by the elbows – cried out exultingly, 'He's fired! I heered him!' and I
50   nodded at the old gentleman until it is no figure of speech to declare that I absolutely could not see him.

From *Great Expectations* by Charles Dickens (1861)

>> Task 8.1

1. Summarise what you learn about Wemmick's old father from this passage. Include:

   - his health
   - his relationship with his son
   - his feelings.

2. Explain why Wemmick does not want his home life 'professionally spoken about'.

3. There is an expression 'an Englishman's home is his castle'. What do you think this means and how does it relate to this passage? Talk about this with a partner before you write your answer. Discuss:

   - why the cottage is referred to as The Castle
   - the meaning and implications of the phrase 'pitch of perfection'
   - Wemmick's attitude to his home
   - the 'nightly ceremony'.

Passage B

1

Basil Street Blues is a personal memoir by the biographer Sir Michael Holroyd. In it he looks back at his boyhood and tries to make sense of the adults in his life, many of whom were colourful characters. For much of his childhood Holroyd was left most of the time with grandparents and his aunt, their daughter, in Berkshire while his separated parents went their own ways. Here he describes how it was at the beginning and paints a vivid word picture of his grandfather.

'What shall we do with the boy?' That cry comes back to me whenever I think of my early years at Maidenhead. As if to answer the question, my father, in the intervals from his career in France, would turn up at Norhurst with some devastating present – an air rifle, chemistry set, conjuring tricks or even golf clubs – and after a few flourishes and gestures, a few words of encouragement and a laugh, leave the fine tuning of my tuition as rifleman, chemist, magician or golfer to my aunt while he returned to fight the

20 Germans or encourage the French. My aunt did her best, but I remember thinking one rainy day as we carried out some lumps of ice to put on her forehead while waiting for the ambulance to arrive, that we shouldn't have chosen the dining room to play cricket.

Most of these events passed my grandfather by. He got little sleep at night and would catch up during the day with a series of 'forty winks'. Besides he had his own disasters to occupy him. The post would arrive, he would shake his head and on the backs of envelopes begin a sequence of calculations that never seemed to come out well. Distracted, he would suddenly stand up and crash his poor head against some unexpected corner of furniture and then, blaming the government and all its works, stick on another piece of Elastoplast.

This Elastoplast, like the impasto of an expressionist painter, covered the dome of my grandfather's head which, because he was bald and somewhat bent, he appeared to be accusingly presenting to us all. His face too, with its changing surface of bumps and bruises, was something of a battlefield largely because of his shaving habits. He was not a skilful shaver. His chin and cheeks, as well as his nose and neck, were sometimes dotted with tufts of cotton wool and crossed with thin red lines like Martian canals. Late in life my father gave him an electric razor. After some experimentation in the privacy of the garage, he found this gadget easiest to use while standing on the seat of the upstairs lavatory from where he plugged its dangling cord into the overhead light. In the darkness the whole operation lasted nearly half-an-hour, for he sometimes submerged part of the kit in the cistern. It was impossible for the rest of us to use the lavatory over these periods. My aunt, my grandmother, Old Nan and myself would line up outside, rattling the door handle and crying out in exasperation. But he felt protected by the comfortable whining of his machine. Occasionally he would shave the same side of his face twice since there was no soap to guide him. But over a week things would even out.

From time to time, amid panic and pandemonium, my grandfather was required to travel up to London for a meeting of the Rajmai Tea Company, and once or twice gave his neatly-folded copy of *The Times* through the smoke of the hissing engine to the train driver who always touched his cap and nodded his head as he took it. My grandfather always came back looking worried from these days in London, and the dogs themselves would sneak into the corners of the rooms.

Part of his difficulties arose from increasing deafness, though this also afforded him protection from the perpetual squabbling that filled the rooms at Norhurst. As a child I had the double experience of my parents' marriage that had unhappily broken up, and my grandparents' marriage that had been unhappily kept going. At one point I was tempted to make an attempt to run away from Maidenhead to join my mother in London; at another point, I attempted to run back from London to Maidenhead. The family was baffled: but I do not feel so baffled.

Norhurst was to be my intermittent home for twenty years.

From *Basil Street Blues* by Michael Holroyd (1999)

143

>> Task 8.2

1. What do you learn from this passage about Holroyd's aunt? Answer as fully as you can.

2. Do you think Holroyd had a happy childhood? Explain you answer with close reading to what he writes or hints at.

3. Like Wemmick's 'Aged Parent' in Passage A, Holroyd's grandfather is deaf. What do the two men have in common and in what ways are they different. Write a detailed answer.

4. This passage is intended to be funny.

   a. How funny do you find it?

   b. Do you find it more or less humorous than Passage A?

   c. What makes these passages witty – one fictional and one a factual memoir?

Passage C

Newspaper obituaries are usually about famous people or important achievers. This one is different. It is about an elderly eccentric who had become so well known in his own area that he had, in a sense, turned into a celebrity. The interest in him is partly because no one really knows the truth about Mr Stawinoga's past or why he behaved as he did, as the obituarist makes clear.

Josef Stawinoga, who died on October 28 aged 86, was a hermit who lived for nearly 40 years in a tent on the central reservation of the A4150 Wolverhampton inner ring road – between PC World and a bathroom showroom.

The Polish-born Stawinoga, known locally as Fred, Trampee or Shakespeare, arrived in Britain after the Second World War, settled in Wolverhampton and dropped out of normal society for unknown reasons sometime in the 1960s. By the 1970s he had moved into a makeshift tent of plastic sheeting erected underneath a weeping willow on the ring road, where he was allowed to remain by the local council.

Unkempt and dirty, with long matted hair and a 2ft straggly, yellowish beard, he became a local celebrity. He was revered by local Hindus and Sikhs as a saint who had shunned all worldly possessions, was awarded an honorary degree by

Wolverhampton Polytechnic and even had his own 6,500-strong fan group – 'we love you Wolverhampton ring-road tramp' – on the internet site Facebook.

25 Local folklore offered several explanations for Stawinoga's chosen way of life. Some claimed he had served as a lance-corporal in the Polish Army Medical Corps and had developed a fear of confined spaces after being detained as a prisoner of war by the Russians. Certainly his well-attested dislike of anyone in uniform seemed to support this theory.

30 Some suggested he chose a solitary life after a failed love affair. Others thought that he might be undergoing a self-imposed penance for something he had done during the war.

On the occasions he did emerge from his haven, it was usually to pick up a brush and sweep the surrounding streets.

35 After his death, a 'friend' claimed that Stawinoga had served in the German Wehrmacht as a member of the SS, 'and he was not one of the nicest chaps in the SS'.

Josef Stawinoga was born on December 15 1920. Little is known about his early life until he arrived in Britain after the war. He worked briefly as a hospital orderly in Wales before finding a job at the steelworks in Bilston. In 1952 he married an Austrian woman with whom he lived in a single room in a boarding house.

40 By all accounts it was not a happy relationship: Stawinoga was said to have taken to locking up his wife when he went to work. She would cry and scream until one day, several years later, a neighbour smashed down the door to let her out. She fled, presumably to Austria.

During the 1960s Stawinoga became increasingly eccentric. Before he moved into his
45 tent he was evicted from nine lodging houses for not paying his rent, and he was often seen pushing a pram containing all his worldly goods. In 1967 he failed to turn up for work. Stawinoga rejected all attempts by the council to rehouse him and eventually the authorities sanctioned his unorthodox living arrangements, arranging for nine replacement tents to be erected over the original plastic sheeting to keep the rain out.

50 Though he did not have a bath in 30 years he never went short of the essentials. Every day members of the local Asian community would come to pay homage with gifts of blankets, clothing and food – including, on one occasion, a live chicken which took up residence inside the tent until it vanished, probably under the wheels of a passing car.

Despite the mystery surrounding his activities in the war, Wolverhampton City
55 Council is said to be planning a memorial service for Stawinoga, and fans have set up a fund to raise money for a statue or plaque in his memory to be erected on the ring road; £200 has already been collected.

From *The Daily Telegraph*, 17th November 2007

Task 8.3

1. Summarise Josef Stawinoga's life in two sentences.

2. What does the writer mean by 'local folklore'? Give examples.

3. How did Stawinoga become 'increasingly eccentric'? Answer as fully as you can.

4. Why do you think Stawinoga became such a well-known and tolerated personality in Wolverhampton?

Passage D

In Greek mythology Tithonus was the lover of Eos, the goddess of the dawn. She bore him a son Memnon. Desperate for his father to live on, Memnon begged Zeus, the leader of the Gods, for the gift of immortality for Tithonus. But he forgot to ask for eternal youth to go with it. So Tithonus is condemned to live for ever, but growing older, iller and more unhappy without the blessing of death to relieve him. Here Alfred Tennyson (1809-1892) gives us an imaginative account of how Tithonus would have felt. The poem is narrated by Tithonus so, in a sense, it is a dramatic monologue as well as a poem, addressed to Eos.

Tithonus

1
The woods decay, the woods decay and fall,
The vapours weep their burthen to the ground,
Man comes and tills the field and lies beneath,
And after many a summer dies the swan.

5
Me only cruel immortality
Consumes; I wither slowly in thine arms,
Here at the quiet limit of the world,
A white-hair'd shadow roaming like a dream
The ever-silent spaces of the East,

10
Far-folded mists, and gleaming halls of morn.

Alas! for this grey shadow, once a man –
So glorious in his beauty and thy choice,
Who madest him thy chosen, that he seem'd
To his great heart none other than a God!
15 I ask'd thee, 'Give me immortality.'
Then didst thou grant mine asking with a smile,
Like wealthy men who care not how they give.
But thy strong Hours indignant work'd their wills,
And beat me down and marr'd and wasted me,
20 And tho' they could not end me, left me maim'd
To dwell in presence of immortal youth,
Immortal age beside immortal youth,
And all I was in ashes. Can thy love,
Thy beauty, make amends, tho' even now,
25 Close over us, the silver star, thy guide,
Shines in those tremulous eyes that fill with tears
To hear me? Let me go: take back thy gift:
Why should a man desire in any way
To vary from the kindly race of men,
30 Or pass beyond the goal of ordinance
Where all should pause, as is most meet for all?

A soft air fans the cloud apart; there comes
A glimpse of that dark world where I was born.
Once more the old mysterious glimmer steals
35 From any pure brows, and from thy shoulders pure,
And bosom beating with a heart renew'd.
Thy cheek begins to redden thro' the gloom,
Thy sweet eyes brighten slowly close to mine,
Ere yet they blind the stars, and the wild team
40 Which love thee, yearning for thy yoke, arise,
And shake the darkness from their loosen'd manes,
And beat the twilight into flakes of fire.

Lo! ever thus thou growest beautiful
In silence, then before thine answer given
45 Departest, and thy tears are on my cheek.
Why wilt thou ever scare me with thy tears,
And make me tremble lest a saying learnt,
In days far-off, on that dark earth, be true?
'The Gods themselves cannot recall their gifts.'

50   Ay me! ay me! with what another heart
In days far-off, and with what other eyes
I used to watch – if I be he that watch'd –
The lucid outline forming round thee; saw
The dim curls kindle into sunny rings;
55   Changed with thy mystic change, and felt my blood
Glow with the glow that slowly crimson'd all
Thy presence and thy portals, while I lay,
Mouth, forehead, eyelids, growing dewy-warm
With kisses balmier than half-opening buds
60   Of April, and could hear the lips that kiss'd
Whispering I knew not what of wild and sweet,
Like that strange song I heard Apollo sing,
While Ilion like a mist rose into towers.

   Yet hold me not for ever in thine East:
65   How can my nature longer mix with thine?
Coldly thy rosy shadows bathe me, cold
Are all thy lights, and cold my wrinkled feet
Upon thy glimmering thresholds, when the steam
Floats up from those dim fields about the homes
70   Of happy men that have the power to die,
And grassy barrows of the happier dead.
Release me, and restore me to the ground;
Thou seest all things, thou wilt see my grave:
Thou wilt renew thy beauty morn by morn!
75   I earth in earth forget these empty courts,
And thee returning on thy silver wheels.

'Tithonius' by Alfred (Lord) Tennyson (1859)

>> Task 8.4

1. Explain – with short quotations from the poem woven into your sentences
   (in inverted commas) – what Tithonus means by 'Me only cruel immortality/consumes'.

2. Choose and comment on three phrases which emphasise Tithonus's terrible ageing.

3. How does Tennyson convey Eos's beauty? Answer as fully as you can using short
   quotations to support your points.

Passage E

Poet Elizabeth Jennings (1926-2001) was the Oxford-educated daughter of a Lincolnshire doctor. By a strange coincidence her background links her with Tennyson (Passage D) who also came from Lincolnshire. Her output of poems was large, although when she was young she also worked as a librarian and later for a publisher. Jennings's obituarist in The Guardian wrote that she developed a 'personal voice' and a 'deceptively simple style'. Here she records, and reflects on, her feelings about elderly people she has observed in a residential home.

Old People's Nursing Home

1   The men have ceased to be men, the women, women.
Or so it appears at first.
Here are children dressed for a meal, napkins in collars,
Here are meals from the nursery, here is the nurse.
5   So it appears to one who is half
Within this house and half outside.
'It will be calm', someone suggested.

And so it seemed at first – tidy and calm
With the weather outside tidy and calm,
10   The carpets, pressed to the walls, forbidding noise,
No smell of a hospital, no smell at all,
And that was what I longed for first, the scent
Of a hyacinth bypassing sickness and pungent with growth,
Perfume thrust on the wrist and rising in clouds
15   In circles of foreign summers.

But there was no smell, not even the deathly sick
Odour of death. And then I realised:
Death is shut from this house, the language of death,
The accoutrements of dying.
20   A ghost would be lively. Ghosts are not allowed here
And neither is talk of birth.

The faces differentiate themselves,
The men half-women, the women half-men
And each entirely children
25   Except in anger, except in ignorance.

These wrinkled faces know too much, these gnarled
Hands have touched the pulse of love, have known
The family increase and birth's harvesting.

But that was the past and this house has shut out the past
30 And it dare not face the future:
So it lives in a perilous present that could be cracked
By a broken cup or a laugh.
Cups are unbreakable here,
And the noisy future, the passionate are dammed
35 Partly by deafness, partly
By doctors' decisions and nurses'
Hiding the stuff of life away –
Tear-heavy handkerchiefs, the whiff of pain.

40 And I who carry compassion find it useless,
I who am very young here feel part-guilty,
Part-helpless. Most, out of place.
For my past and future spread throughout my present,
Time is a scheme of light and dark,
45 'What is the time?' an old woman whispers.
Nobody answers and I,
With a load of compassion to scatter, refuse to tell her
For to do so would set the rainbow over this house,
Of movements and mornings which lead to death, and death
50 Is an outcast here for a night, an hour, for how long?

'Old People's Nursing Home' by Elizabeth Jennings (1977)

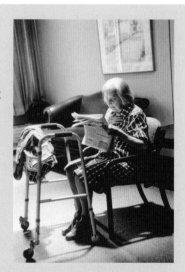

Task 8.5

1. Summarise life in the nursing home. Use your own words incorporating short quotations putting them in inverted commas.

2. In what ways are the nursing home residents 'children' or 'entirely children'?

3. What does the poet mean by 'a perilous present' (line 31) and why does she find it so difficult? Answer as fully as you can and include short quotations from the poem in your answer.

4. Discuss with a partner what, if anything, Passage D has in common with Passage E and the ways in which the poems differ. Consider:

- the narrator's role in the poem
- the subject matter of each poem
- the pattern of the lines and their rhythm
- use of rhyme or lack of it
- how rhythm and rhyme adds to meaning
- anything else which interests you.

Now write a detailed comparison of the two poems.

Passage F

1   King Lear is, for many people, Shakespeare's most profound play. It is about an old man – an elderly king – and how he has to live
5   with the consequences of an irresponsible decision. In some ways it is a family story about Lear's relationship with his adult daughters, but on another level it is much
10 more. Most critics were very impressed with the Royal Shakespeare Company's (RSC) 2007/8 production with Sir Ian McKellen in the title role. But this reviewer, writing for The
15 Stage – the performing arts profession's own newspaper – has reservations. Notice what a lot he packs into a very few words.

The RSC King Lear starts off unpromisingly, with an interpolated grand procession in Ruritanian costume to loud organ music.

It quickly settles down, however, to a rather conventional, almost textbook reading of the play. The love test is a scripted charade, and Romola Garai's Cordelia is startled that her impulsive and half-joking ad libs so enrage the king. The elder sisters are familiar characterisations, Frances Barber's imperious and oily Goneril balanced by Monica Dolan's more impulsive and, here, hard-drinking Regan.

Jonathan Hyde's Kent is angular and forceful, driven by the conviction of his righteousness, Sylvester McCoy's Fool is the by now standard half-weeping older man, and William Gaunt supplies almost the only real warmth and humanity in the play as Gloucester. Philip Winchester has to fight the temptation to twirl his

Ian McKellan as King Lear at the Courtyard Theatre, Stratford upon Avon, 2007

25   mustachios in melodramatic villainy as Edmund, though Ben Meyjes does show Edgar
growing from shallow bookworm to strong and feeling hero through his ordeal.

At the centre, Ian McKellen walks through the first half of the play, bringing little to
the table. His characterisation deepens after the storm scene, showing a mind and
heart in Lear that utilises madness as a learning experience to come out with greater
30   wisdom and modesty.

Dover beach, the awakening, the off-to-prison speech and the final scene are as
moving as anyone could wish, though always wholly within the bounds of previous
productions and interpretations, and repeatedly giving the sense that, at their best,
director Trevor Nunn and his actors have stayed out of the way of the play's inherent
35   power rather than adding much to it.

By Gerald Berkowitz, *The Stage*, 29th November 2007

›› Task 8.6

Summarise Gerald Berkowitz's views about this production. Quote briefly from the
passage (using inverted commas) to support your points.

Writing about literature

Here is an example of how you might write critically about the language used in an obituary. This is an extract from Passage C.

> Josef Stawinoga was born on December 15 1920. Little is known about his early life until he arrived in Britain after the war. He worked briefly as a hospital orderly in Wales before finding a job at the steelworks in Bilston. In 1952 he married an Austrian woman with whom he lived in a single room in a boarding house.

This paragraph is carefully factual, unlike much of the rest of the obituary which is speculative because no one knows the truth. First the obituarist makes a simple, inarguable statement about Stawinoga's birth putting the subject of the sentence first for clarity. Then he jumps to what happened after his subject's arrival in Britain and gives three facts in chronological order: his work first in a hospital then in a steelworks and finally his marriage. Because the writer is concentrating on facts here there are almost no adjectives and adverbs to clutter the text apart from the ones (such as 'early', 'Austrian', 'single', 'briefly') which are essential to meaning. The elegance and accessibility comes from deliberately chosen, straightforward nouns and verbs such as 'arrived', 'worked', 'lived', 'job' and 'room'. Almost every word is short and to the point.

Personal Writing

>> Task 8.7

1. Write a story in which an elderly man or woman is the main character.

2. Write an obituary suitable for a newspaper of any elderly person you know (or know of) who has recently died – it could be a member of your family, a friend, neighbour or someone in public life. It could even be someone you 'know' from fiction.

3. Write a review of any of the books suggested in the 'Wide Range Reading' section of this or any other chapter of this book. Make it about the same length (250 to 300 words) as Gerald Berkowitz's play review of *King Lear*. Do not waste words – get as much information into your space as you can.

4. Write a poem about any aspect of old age.

5. In Britain many elderly people end their lives in nursing homes where specialist care is available. Alternatively, they might be cared for at home by family members. The latter way is usual in, for example, Muslim countries. Write an essay setting out which way you think is best and explain your reasons. Use any personal knowledge you have and bring in anecdotes (little stories from your own experience) if you wish.

> ## >> Task 8.7 (cont.)
>
> 6. Write about a colourful and interesting elderly person who is known to you.
>
> ___
>
> 7. Write about old age in any way you wish.

Writing tip

When you want to write a personal impression of someone start with a blank sheet of plain A4 paper. Put the person's name in a circle in the middle. Now jot at random elsewhere on the sheet words and phrases which describe him or her such as 'not a skilful shaver' and 'red lines like Martian canals'. Then, in a different colour, add the things about him or her that you particularly want to mention – as Michael Holroyd did with his grandfather's collisions with the furniture and his business trips to London. This is your raw material. Now, on another sheet of paper, decide how you are going to order it by working out what you will mention in each paragraph. This is your plan. Now write the piece.

WORD BANK

In Passage A Michael Holroyd uses the word **pandemonium**. Coined by John Milton (1608–1674) in his epic poem 'Paradise Lost', the word originally meant **many devils** or **hell** from the Ancient Greek words *pan* (all) and *daimon* (devil or demon). Today it is usually used to mean **chaos**, **muddle** or **noise**.

Wemmick takes Pip to sit in an **arbour** in passage B. It means **a leafy glade shaded by trees** and Dickens is joking gently because Wemmick's is only a small cottage garden which has (probably) just one tree. An arbour – quite old fashioned even in Dickens's time – would normally be larger and, perhaps part of a park or estate. It comes from the Latin word *arbor* (tree).

> ## >> Task 8.8
>
> Look up the meanings of the following ten words all of which derive from *pan*, *daimon* or *arbor*. Make a note on each to help you remember it.
>
> | | |
> |---|---|
> | panorama | panacea |
> | arboretum | arborescent |
> | pandemic | panoply |
> | demonise | arboreal |
> | arborist | demonic |

>> Task 8.9

Use each of these words – taken from the passages above – in sentences of your own to show that you understand their meaning. Change the part of speech or the verb/noun ending if you wish. (That is use 'bestir' or 'bestirred' and so on instead of 'bestirring' if you prefer, for example.)

Then work with a partner testing each other until you can both spell them all:

1.	bestirring	6.	penance	11.	compassion
2.	devastating	7.	homage	12.	interpolated
3.	intermittent	8.	lucid	13.	inherent
4.	revered	9.	accoutrements	14.	differentiate
5.	attested	10.	perilous	15.	gnarled

NUTS AND BOLTS

Adverbial clauses and phrases

In Chapter 7 (page 133) we looked at complex sentences and how they are constructed. We saw how noun phrases and adjectival phrases and clauses work.

Now we take that further with adverbial phrases and clauses.

An adverb is, of course, a word which qualifies (or modifies) a verb or, occasionally, an adjective or another adverb.

An adverbial clause or phrase is a group of words which functions in a sentence like an adverb. Look at the following examples:

Some suggested he chose a solitary life **after a failed love affair**.

(An adverb such as 'later' or 'reluctantly' would fit in place of the adverbial clause (in bold) which qualifies the verb 'chose'. The adverbial phrase 'after a failed love affair' explains when he made the choice.)

That cry comes back to me **whenever I think of my early years at Maidenhead**.

(The adverbial clause – complete with its own full verb 'think' qualifies the sentence's main verb 'comes'. It tells us when the thought comes. You could substitute an adverb such as 'often' or 'occasionally' for the adverbial clause in this sentence and it would still make sense.)

Adverbial clauses and phrases often start with a preposition such as 'after' or 'whenever'. The above examples both relate to time. But there are three other main sorts of adverbials. Identify them according to the questions they answer:

1. An adverbial clause of manner answers the question 'How'? For example:

    As she reluctantly did every morning, she reached for her school uniform.

    Or an adverbial phrase of manner:

    Showing her reluctance, she reached for her school uniform.

2. An adverbial clause of place answers the question 'Where'? For example:

    Migrants settle **wherever they can find jobs**.

    Or an adverbial phrase of place:

    Migrants settle **in areas with jobs**.

3. An adverbial clause of reason answers the question 'Why'? For example:

    I lent her my textbook **because she had forgotten hers**.

    Or an adverbial phrase of reason:

    I lent her my textbook **because of her forgetfulness**.

4. An adverbial clause of time (which we have already met) answers the question 'When'? For example:

    When it stops raining we shall go for a walk.

    Or an adverbial phrase of time:

    After the rain we shall go for a walk.

>> Task 8.10

Write eight sentences to practise your use of adverbial clauses. Write two each for manner, place, reason and time.

Then try rewriting them using a phrase instead of a clause. Try to retain the main sense of your original sentence.

Colons and semi-colons

A **colon** (:) has the meaning **as follows** or **like this** in a sentence. So writers often use them to precede lists. For example:

> While we were in Sainsbury's we bought plenty of fruit: apples, kiwis, nectarines, grapes and two large pineapples.

A colon can also be used to introduce direct speech if the writer needs something stronger than a comma. For example:

> As Wemmick might have said: 'You have to take great care of your aged parents.'

Or you can use it to indicate that important information follows – as I usually do in this book when I'm about to offer you an example!

> For example:

> Many of the people polled in the survey were against it: about thirty percent totally, forty percent mostly and the rest unsure.

A **semi-colon** (;) can be used to separate detailed items in a list when commas are needed within the items. For example:

> At tonight's party we are expecting my elderly aunt, who has lived in Yorkshire all her life and doesn't often get to London; my father's old college friend with his wife and three children, one of whom is disabled; three neighbours from various houses in our road and most of the people my mother works with.

The other main use of the semi-colon is as an alternative to a full stop when two ideas – or would-be separate sentences – are very closely related. For example:

> Trollope was a great novelist; Dickens was greater.

> I like all fruit; mango is my favourite.

Note: the word after a semi-colon should NOT have a capital (upper case) letter unless it is a proper noun.

This use of the semi-colon seems to be disappearing. You rarely see it in newspapers, for example. Some modern novelists still use it, although nothing like as often as Dickens did.

>> Task 8.11

Practise using colons and semi-colons.

Make up several sentences to illustrate the different uses of each.

GET IT RIGHT

Dictation was once a routine exercise in every classroom. Pupils would learn or 'prepare' (hence the word **prep** meaning **homework**) spellings and punctuation in a short passage and then the teacher would read the passage for the class to write as a test. It is now rather out of fashion, which is a pity because it is a useful way of learning.

Try the dictation in Task 8.12 with a partner. First take some time to learn the spellings and the punctuation. Then take it in turns to dictate it to each other.

First read the whole passage clearly to your partner. Then break it down into three or four word blocks reading each twice to give him or her time to write it. At the end read it straight through at normal speed so that your partner can check his or her work.

>> Task 8.12

Dictation passage

We were searching for reasonably priced accommodation in the village: the choice was severely limited. We tried to ignore the appalling decorative state of some of the buildings we viewed but we discovered that nicely carpeted floors and prettily papered walls did have an effect on our attitude. Finally we bought a thatched cottage: pitifully neglected. We enjoyed restoring it to its former character. We hammered; we chiselled; we levelled. We laboured all that autumn and by Christmas we were beginning to believe it would never be finished. However, nobody regretted the decision to buy, despite the colossal mortgage.

Passage adapted from *A Guide to Better Spelling* by AM Burt, Stanley Thornes (Publishers) Ltd (1982).

More speaking and listening activities

With your teacher's permission invite an older person into your classroom to answer questions about his or her experiences and how things have changed. Work out your questions by discussing them in groups in advance.

Interview an elderly person. Ask him or her about their earliest memories. Listen very carefully and/or use a recorder and/or take notes. Then summarise what you have learned and share it with a small group in your class.

Do you think elderly people are treated with the respect they deserve? Organise a class discussion to consider this.

Read one of more of the books in the 'Wide Range Reading' section of this chapter. Tell the rest of the class about it in the form of an oral review.

Working with two others make a short play (often called a 'sketch') of Pip's first visit to Wemmick's home in Passage A.

With a partner prepare and rehearse a reading of one of the poems in this section. Then perform it to the rest of the class.

Here is another initials quiz. This time it is poems and poets. For example:

Clue: TROTAM by STC

Answer: 'The Rime of the Ancient Mariner' by Samuel Taylor Coleridge

Clue: HR by TH

Answer: 'Hawk Roosting' by Ted Hughes

All the poems here are ones which you are likely already to have read in school or seen in anthologies.

1. TH by AN
2. TLOS by ALT (sometimes known as LT or AT)
3. TPPOH by RB
4. TOATPC by EL
5. SF by JM

6. D by WW
7. O by PBS
8. TT by WB
9. TL by WDLM
10. DEDE by WO

WIDE RANGE READING

The Lady in the Van by Alan Bennett (1999). Miss Mary Shepherd was a strange, elderly eccentric who liked to park the van in which she lived in the street in London where playwright Alan Bennett lives. In the end he invited her to park it on his drive, never expecting her to stay for many years. The book tells the extraordinary – very funny but also often sad – true story of Bennett's relationship with Miss Shepherd. He has also written this as a very successful play which first ran in London with Maggie Smith as Miss Shepherd. Other productions of it have been put on elsewhere since.

The Picture of Dorian Gray by Oscar Wilde (1891). Wilde's spooky novel tells the story of Gray whose portrait showed him as a handsome young man. So determined was Gray not to age that he wished for the face in the painting to grow old while he remained young. In one of the more macabre stories in English, Gray gets his wish … until the end of the story which is pretty dramatic. Compare it with 'The Ballad of Reading Gaol' (in Chapter 1, page 6) or with any of Wilde's plays or short stories.

Diary of an Ordinary Woman by Margaret Forster (2003). The narrator of this novel is given the diary of a woman who has just died aged 98. She is asked to edit it for publication. The result is a splendid story-within-a-story about a woman who was 13 when the First World War started in 1914. She lives through almost the entire 20th century so we see her during two wars and dealing with many problems and encounters. It's a very compelling read – like all Margaret Forster's novels.

Mrs Dalloway by Virginia Woolf (1925). Mrs Clarissa Dalloway, who is not young, lives in London and she has decided to hold a party. The novel is about the lead-up to the party, what Mrs Dalloway does and the thoughts she has during the day. Virginia Woolf – and other writers such as James

Joyce – were experimenting with new ways of writing in the 1920s. Instead of telling a straightforward story they tried to describe the random nature of what goes on in characters' minds. This style is sometimes called 'stream of consciousness'. Mrs Dalloway is beautifully written. Each paragraph is like a crisp little jewel.

Last Orders by Graham Swift (1996). Four elderly friends who drink together in a London pub are mourning the death of another friend, the butcher, Jack Dodds. It was Jack's wish that his ashes should be scattered in the sea. So (a bit like Chaucer's pilgrims) they drive through Kent to Margate for a day out – with the ashes. This is a fine story about friendship and dealing with old age and death. It was made into a good film too. You might like to watch a DVD of the film after you've read the book and work out which you prefer and why.

The Summer of a Dormouse by John Mortimer (2000). Mortimer, who died in 2009, was a barrister, novelist, playwright and author of the TV series *Rumpole of the Bailey.* He subtitled this witty book 'a year of growing old disgracefully'. Almost to his death, Mortimer continued going to parties, gossiping and joking, about his difficulties. For him, age was certainly 'just a state of mind'. Like all Mortimer's writing, this is a very entertaining and cheeful book.

- **Many wonderful poems have been written about old age and death. Read 'Blue Gentians' by DH Lawrence (1885–1930). 'Do not go gentle into that good night' by Dylan Thomas (1914–1953) and 'Elegy Written in a Country Churchyard' by Thomas Gray (1716–1771), for example. Look for others and create your own themed anthology.**

- **Find out about the work of the charity Help the Aged. You could then organise an assembly on its work and/or (with your teacher's permission) invite a speaker from Help the Aged to talk to your class or school.**

- **Read *Great Expectations*. Decide whether you think Dickens's portrayal (through Pip's narration) is patronising or affectionate – or something else?**

Read and make a study of *King Lear*. It is one of the most thoughtful pieces of literature ever written about ageing and how it affects people. The easiest way to read a play is aloud with a partner – taking it in turn to read the parts. Then, or instead, you might listen to an audio version or watch a film of the play on DVD. The version which Laurence Olivier starred in and directed (1983) is still one of the best. Better still, of course, take the opportunity to see a live performance if you can.

How do you feel when suddenly you understand something you didn't understand before? Or you make a discovery? Most of us feel pretty pleased. When I discovered recently that the word **companion** originally meant **someone with whom you broke bread** I grinned and couldn't wait to share it with someone. Sometimes I cheer when I learn something new which pleases me. Or when I see something which I have heard about all my life but never before seen – such as the Leaning Tower of Pisa or the Sphinx – it has the same effect on me. How about you?

These are sometimes called our 'eureka' moments. The word comes from the Greek *heurika* – I have it. It is what the Greek mathematician Archimedes is supposed to have shouted when he leaped from his bath (see Passage C) in the excitement of his discovery.

In this chapter we start with several people's eureka moments in different genres of writing. First there's an extract from the *Oxford Dictionary of National Biography*, then an obituary, some factual writing for children, a couple of very different pieces of poetry and a fiction extract.

Passage A

The Dictionary of National Biography was a huge, late 19th century publication in 63 volumes. Various supplements to it were published during the 20th century to cover people who had recently died. Then in the late 1980s Oxford University Press decided to redo the whole work – a massive task. The result, the Oxford Dictionary of National Biography, which tells the life story of 56,000 people and involved 10,000 contributors, was published in 2004. It is easier to update it now because editors can add to it online. Most people can refer to it free from any computer via the website of their local public library as long as they have a library card, although big libraries have it in traditional book form as well. Each entry in the ODNB is written to a very specific brief as this shortened version of the entry on Alexander Fleming, discoverer of penicillin, shows.

1   Fleming, Sir Alexander (1881–1955), bacteriologist and discoverer of penicillin, was born on 6 August 1881, the third of the four children of Hugh Fleming (d. 1888), farmer, of Lochfield, in the parish of Loudoun near Darvel, in Ayrshire, from his second marriage to Grace Sterling Morton (d. 1928), the daughter of a neighbouring

5   farmer. Hugh Fleming, whose ancestors probably came from the Low Countries, had four surviving children from his first marriage. He was sixty at the time of his second marriage, and died when Alexander (known as Alec) was seven.

Alec Fleming's early education was in a small country school at Loudoun Moor, then at Darvel School, and finally for eighteen months at Kilmarnock Academy. He won

10   the senior entrance scholarship in natural science at St Mary's London, and many
other class prizes and scholarships during his student career. He qualified as a doctor
and took the conjoint qualification in 1908. With a very good memory, learning was
seldom a burden. However, his life was never all work and no play; both as an
undergraduate and as a postgraduate he was an active and proficient member of the
15   swimming, shooting, and golf clubs, and even took some part in the drama society.
Fleming had a natural combativeness and urge to win which were very apparent in
the games he played. This determination to succeed was also evident in his medical
and laboratory work, where he took delight in using his technical skill and
inventiveness to overcome difficulties.

20   While Fleming's name became synonymous with penicillin and the antibiotic
revolution of the late 1940s and early 1950s, later assessments have given more
weight to the work of other scientists, most notably Chain and Florey, and to the
teams in the United States that produced penicillin on an industrial scale. There is
also a fascination with what Fleming himself called the Fleming myth. That is why
25   and how a single scientist was ever made responsible for the discovery of penicillin
and how a reserved hospital bacteriologist became an international celebrity.

In September 1928 Fleming made the world-famous observation of a mould
inhibiting the growth of bacteria which has been seen as the beginning of the
antibiotic era in the treatment of infections. Fleming was studying colony variation in
30   the staphylococcus, the germ that causes septic infections, for a chapter he was
writing for the System of Bacteriology. On his return from a holiday he noticed on a
discarded plate culture that the micro-organism was absent from an area around a
contaminating mould. The contaminant was *Penicillium notatum*, a common mould
found across the world. Fleming was more interested in the phenomenon than were
35   his colleagues. He presumed that the contamination was accidental and that the
mould had entered his laboratory through an open window. He worked with the
mould and its 'juice' for the next six months. Fleming first spoke on this work to the
Medical Research Club on 13 February 1929 and submitted his first paper to the
British Journal of Experimental Pathology on 10 May. It appeared a month later.

40   There has been much debate on why the therapeutic potential of penicillin was not
recognized in 1929. Through the 1930s Fleming used penicillin in a small number of
cases as a local antiseptic and as a laboratory reagent for selective culturing, as did a
number of other clinicians.

In 1938 and 1939 the Oxford group working on germicides began to home in on
45   penicillin. The first experiments with intravenous injections of penicillin on infected
mice began in May 1940, with their very promising results published in August.
Fleming visited Oxford to catch up with the work in September, seemingly curious
about the applications being made with 'his juice'. A year later, after publication of
the results of the first extremely promising clinical trials, Fleming first made public his

50 proprietorial claims to penicillin. He crossed swords in print with the Oxford group, claiming that as well as having discovered the antibacterial properties of the substance he had
55 recognized its potential as a systemic antibacterial drug. This contretemps in the medical press brought media attention to penicillin.

The high profile given to penicillin
60 changed Fleming's standing in science and medicine. On 18 March 1943 he was elected a Fellow of the Royal Society, a position he had sought for some twenty years. In 1944 he was
65 made a Fellow of the Royal College of

Sir Alexander Fleming by Ethel Gabain (1883-1950)

Physicians and knighted, and in October 1945 he received, with Florey and Chain, the Nobel prize for physiology and medicine. Fleming became head of the newly-named Wright-Fleming Institute, but he was more often than not away receiving many and varied accolades. He travelled widely in Europe and throughout the Americas, north
70 and south, as further prizes were awarded, honorary degrees by the dozen were conferred, statues were unveiled, freedom of cities granted, and streets named in his honour. Among the most notable awards were: Commander of the Légion d'honneur in France, Member of the Pontifical Academy of Sciences, election as Rector of the University of Edinburgh (1951–4), convocation member of the senate of the
75 University of London from 1950, member of the Medical Research Council (1945–9), and President of the Society for General Microbiology (1945–7). Besides becoming an honorary citizen of numerous cities in Europe he was a freeman of the burgh of Darvel, where he was born, and of the London boroughs of Chelsea, where he lived, and of Paddington, where his work was done.

80 In October 1949 Fleming's wife, Sareen, died. In the succeeding years Fleming continued to travel, becoming close to Amalia Vourekas, née Coutsouris (b. 1912/13), daughter of Harilaos Coutsouris, a physician. She was a medically qualified bacteriologist who had joined the institute in 1946. They eventually married on 9 April 1953. Fleming died suddenly from a heart attack at his home in Danvers Street,
85 Chelsea, on 11 March 1955, in the middle of a busy schedule. He was cremated and his ashes interred in London in St Paul's Cathedral a week later.

Abridged and slightly adapted from an article by Michael Warboys in *Oxford Dictionary of National Biography* (2004)

>> Task 9.1

1. Write the four facts which seem to you most important about Alexander Fleming's life. Use four short sentences.

2. Explain in your own words – but in as much detail as you can – the accidental discovery of 1929 and why it was so important.

3. Summarise in a short passage what you learn from the passage about Fleming's family life.

4. Why did the story of Fleming's discovery become so well known?

Passage B

Eve Curie's mother, Marie and her father, Pierre Curie, were the discoverers of radioactivity which led to a whole new branch of science. Jointly they won the Nobel Prize for physics in 1903 and Marie won it again in 1911, after Pierre's death, for her discovery of radium. Their elder daughter Irene followed her parents into science. The younger, Eve, did other things with her life and lived to a very great age as this obituary shows. Compare it with the obituary in Chapter 8 on page 144. Discuss with a partner how obituaries differ from biographical articles such as Passage A.

Eve Curie, who died on October 22 aged 102, was the youngest child of the Nobel prize-winning scientists Pierre and Marie Curie but gained fame in her own terms as a concert pianist, writer and biographer.

As her interests were musical and literary rather than scientific, Eve Curie was the only member of her family who did not win a Nobel Prize.

In 1935 her elder sister Irene, with her husband Frederic Joliot, won the Nobel Prize in chemistry for their synthesis of new radioactive elements. Yet Eve did much to promote her family's scientific reputation and was largely responsible for the creation of the emblematic Girls' Own heroine image of her mother with the triumphal biography she published in 1937.

Eve Curie's account of her mother's life, from her birth and childhood in Poland to her discovery, with her husband, of radioactive radium and polonium, became a bestseller that won the American National Book Award for non-fiction and, in 1943, was made into an MGM film starring Greer Garson as Marie and Walter Pidgeon as Pierre.

Yet later reviewers criticised Eve Curie for covering up the affair which Marie Curie had after her husband's death with Paul Langevin, a former pupil of her husband's and a married man with four children, an affair that had been a huge public scandal in France at the time.

Given when the book was published, and the fact that Eve was writing about her mother, the omission was, perhaps, understandable. But Eve's biography also minimised or ignored the humiliations Marie faced at the hands of the French scientific establishment and the Parisian tabloid press after her husband's death.

Thus, while the biography may have inspired generations of scientifically minded girls to believe that they too could succeed in a male-dominated profession, it did not give them a true picture of the sort of hurdles they might have to overcome.

Eve Denise Curie was born in Paris on December 6 1904, the year after her parents (with Henri Becquerel) won the Nobel Prize for Physics. Her father, Pierre, was killed when she was two after he slipped and fell under the wheels of a carriage.

As a child, Eve saw little of her mother, only becoming close to her as a teenager. In 1921, with her elder sister Irene, she accompanied Marie on a tour of America. After Irene's marriage to Frederic Joliot, Eve lived alone with her mother and nursed her through the leukaemia which eventually killed her in 1934.

Though Eve Curie achieved degrees in science and philosophy at the College Sevigny, her true interests were musical and artistic.

A proficient pianist, she performed her first concert in Paris in 1925 and gave concerts in France and Belgium until the outbreak of war.

Attractive, chic and dark-haired, she attracted as much attention for her beauty as for her playing. She also wrote music, theatre and film reviews under a pseudonym.

In 1940, after the fall of France, Eve Curie went to England to work for the Free French and was appointed head of the women's division of the Commissariat of Information.

Famous, particularly in America, on account of her biography of her mother, she used her public profile to promote the Free French cause on lecture tours. In 1940 an essay, French Women and the War, was published in Atlantic Monthly. In 1943 a series of reports from various battle fronts was published as Journey Among Warriors.

60   Returning to France after the war, Eve Curie became the co-publisher of the daily newspaper Paris Press and in 1952 was appointed a special adviser to the Secretary-General of Nato.

In 1954 she married Henri Labouisse, the American ambassador to Greece, who would serve as executive director of Unicef when it was awarded the Nobel Peace
65   Prize in 1965. She herself served as a director of Unicef in Greece from 1962 to 1965.

After her husband's death in 1987 Eve Curie divided her time between New York, Paris and Greece. She became an American citizen in 1958.

From *The Daily Telegraph*, 17th November 2007

>> Task 9.2

1.   What do you learn from this passage about Eve Curie's famous mother, Marie? Write in as much detail as you can.

2a.   How was Eve Curie different from the rest of her family?

  b.   What did she have in common with them?

3.   Compare this fairly typical newspaper obituary with the fairly standard ODNB entry which is Passage A. Remember that Passage A will be consulted mostly by students, journalists, writers, scientists and so on. Passage B is meant for non-specialist readers in a daily newspaper. Consider:

   • the opening and closing paragraph of each

   • sentence shape

   • paragraphing

   • vocabulary

   • the extent to which each passage is factual or conveys the writer's opinions.

1

5

10

15

20

25

30

35

Passage C

This account of the Greek mathematician, Archimedes and the discovery known for ever after as 'Archimedes's Principle' comes from a children's book. What age group do you think it is aimed at? Look carefully at the language, style and the way it presents information and discuss it with a partner or in a small group. How different is the vocabulary and expression from, say, that of Passages A and B, both of which are intended for adults? If you were the editor of the book this extract comes from how would you illustrate it?

Why do some things float and others sink? This is an important question for ship designers, but the ancient Greek scientist Archimedes may have found the answer while he was checking the quality of the king's jewellery.

Archimedes was born in Syracuse, Sicily, in about 290 BC. He was related to the king, Hieron II, so had plenty of time to think and write about mathematics and mechanics. Hieron often called upon Archimedes to help him with problems. He had a gold wreath which he thought contained some silver and asked Archimedes to find out exactly how much.

Archimedes knew he could check the wreath if he could measure its density (its mass in relation to its volume) because he knew that silver is less dense than gold. The obvious way to find the density of something is to measure its weight (which is proportional to its mass) and volume. But Archimedes didn't know how to measure the volume of a wreath.

One day he noticed the water rising as he got into his bath. He then realised he could fill a bath to the top, lower the wreath into it to make the water overflow, then take the wreath out and see how much water was needed to refill the bath. That quantity would be the volume of the wreath.

Archimedes may also have noticed that he felt lighter in his bath. Left to itself bath water doesn't rise or fall, so every part of it must get an upward push that balances its own weight. The same force must push on anything placed in the water. When anything is immersed in a fluid (liquid or gas), even partly, it feels an upward push equal to the weight of fluid it displaces. We now call this the Archimedes Principle. Archimedes, by using this method, could have immersed the wreath in the water and noted how much weight it lost. He could then have worked out how much silver it contained without measuring its volume at all. Archimedes probably didn't do this.

Nevertheless, he had solved Hieron's problem. He may have discovered why things float or sink. Objects placed in water move downwards until their weight is balanced

40 by the weight of the water they displace and then stay at that level. If their average density is higher than that of water they cannot float. They sink.

45 It is said that Archimedes was so excited by his discovery that he leapt out of his bath and ran naked through the streets shouting 'Eureka!' (I've found it). This probably didn't happen, but people still shout 'Eureka!' at moments of discovery.

50 When Archimedes was an old man Hieron had more serious problems. The Romans were besieging Syracuse. Archimedes used his scientific knowledge to design ships, catapults and, it is said, mirrors to burn Roman ships with the sun's rays. In 211 BC the city was

55 captured. Roman soldiers rampaged through it burning the buildings and killing the people. One of their victims was Archimedes, the genius who did science in his bath.

From 'Doing Science in the Bath' in *1,000 Inventions and Discoveries* by Roger Bridgman (2002)

>> Task 9.3

1. Summarise Archimedes's discoveries in your own words. Write as fully, but as clearly, as you can.

2. What do you learn about Archimedes's life from this passage?

3. Write a comparison of this passage with either Passage A or Passage B (following your discussion suggested above). How can you tell that Passage C was written for children while the others were not? Consider:
   - vocabulary
   - tone (for example, question at the beginning and story telling conventions: 'One day …')
   - sentence length
   - paragraphing
   - assumptions about what the reader is likely to know already
   - entertainment value.

Passage D

William Wordsworth (1770-1850) was one of a small group known afterwards as the 'Romantic poets' because they were interested in feelings and emotions. Among many other things they were excited by the beauty of landscape. Wordsworth lived most all his life in the Lake District in the north-west of England, but during his time at Cambridge as a student he went on a walking tour of France, Germany and Switzerland - and later settled in France for a while. He and his friends were very moved by their crossing of the Alps in 1790 - it was a real discovery for them. Wordsworth's feelings are described here in this extract from his long autobiographical poem 'The Prelude' which was first published in 1805.

1	Yet still in me, mingling with these delights
	Was something of stern mood, an under-thirst
	Of vigour, never utterly asleep.
	Far different dejection once was mine,
5	A deep and genuine sadness then I felt;
	The circumstances here I will relate
	Even as they were. Upturning with a Band
	Of Travellers, from the Valais we had clomb
	Along the road that leads to Italy;
10	A length of hours, making of these our Guides
	Did we advance, and having reach'd an Inn
	Among the mountains, we together ate
	Our noon's repast, from which the Travellers rose,
	Leaving us at the Board. Ere long we follow'd
15	Descending by the beaten road that led
	Right to a rivulet's edge, and there broke off.
	The only track now visible was one
	Upon the further side, right opposite,
	And up a lofty Mountain. This we took
20	After a little scruple, and a short pause,
	And climb'd with eagerness, though not, at length
	Without surprise, and some anxiety
	On finding that we did not overtake
	Our comrades gone before. By fortunate chance,
25	While every moment now encreas'd our doubts,
	A peasant met us, and from him we learn'd

That to the place which had perplex'd us first
We must descend, and there should find the road
Which in the stony channel of the Stream
30   Lay a few steps, and then along its banks;
And further, that thenceforward all our course
Was downwards, with the current of the Stream.
Hard of belief, we question'd him again,
And all the answers which the Man return'd
35   To our inquiries, and in their sense and substance,
Translated by the feelings which we had
Ended in this; that we had cross'd the Alps.

Imagination! Lifting up itself
Before the eye and progress of my Song
40   Like an unfather'd vapour; here that Power,
In all the might of its endowments, came
Athwart me; I was lost as in a cloud,
Halted, without a struggle to break through.
And now recovering, to my Soul I say
45   I recognise thy glory; in such strength
Of usurpation, in such visitings
Of awful promise, when light of sense
Goes out in flashes that hath shewn to us
The invisible world, doth Greatness make abode,
50   There harbours whether we be young or old.
Our destiny, our nature, and our home
Is with infinitude, and only there;
With hope it is, hope can never die,
Effort, and expectation, and desire,
55   And something evermore about to be.
The mind beneath such banners militant
Thinks not of spoils or trophies, nor of aught
That may attest its prowess, blest in thoughts
That are their own perfection and reward,
60   Strong in itself, and in the access of joy
Which hides it like the overflowing Nile.

The dull and heavy slackening that ensued
Upon those tidings by the Peasant given
Was soon dislodg'd; downwards we hurried fast,
65   And enter'd with the road which we had miss'd
Into a narrow chasm; the brook and road

A View of Chamonix and Mont Blanc by Joseph Jansen

Were fellow-travellers in this gloomy Pass,
And with them did we journey several hours
At a slow step. The immeasurable height
70 Of woods decaying, never to be decay'd.
The stationary blasts of water-falls,
And every where along the hollow rent
Winds thwarting winds, bewilder'd and forlorn,
The torrents shooting from the clear blue sky,
75 The rocks that mutter'd close upon our ears,
Black drizzling crags that spake by the way-side
As if a giddy prospect of the raving stream,
The unfetter'd clouds, and region of the Heavens,
Tumult and peace, the darkness and the light
80 Were all like workings of the mind, the features
Of the same face, blossoms upon one tree,
Characters of the great Apocalypse,
The types and symbols of Eternity,
Of first and last, and midst, and without end.

From Book VI of 'The Prelude' by William Wordsworth.

>> Task 9.4

1. How does crossing the Alps make the poet feel? Answer in as much detail as you can and work short quotations (using inverted commas) from the extract into your answer.

2. Explain in your own words what Wordsworth and his companions did and saw in the few hours after they had crossed the Alps.

3. Choose three lines or phrases from this extract which you particularly like or find interesting. Write about them in as much detail as you can.

Passage E

Colin Rowbotham was a special needs teacher and poet. He died in 2000, aged 50, having published two volumes of poetry in his lifetime. Until quite recently dissection - cutting into dead animals to learn about how they work - was a standard part of biology work, particularly at A level. Here the poet explores his feelings about the rat he is working on and the discoveries he is making - not all of them quite what the science teacher probably intended!

Dissection

1   This rat looks like it is made of marzipan
Soft and neatly packaged in its envelope;
I shake it free.
Fingering the damp, yellow fur, I know
5   That this first touch is far the worst.
    There is a book about it that contains
Everything on a rat, with diagrams
Meticulous, but free from blood
Or the yellow juices
10   I will have to pour away.
    Now peg it out:
My pins are twisted and the board is hard
But, using force and fracturing its legs
I manage though
15   And crucify my rat.
    From the crutch to the throat the fur is ripped

Not neatly, not as shown in the diagrams,
But raggedly;
My hacking has revealed the body wall
20   As a sack that is fat with innards to be torn
By the inquisitive eye
And the hand that strips aside.
    Inside this taut, elastic sack is a surprise;
Not the chaos that I had thought to find,
25   No oozing mash; instead of that
A firmly coiled discipline
Of overlapping liver, folded gut;
A neatness that is like a small machine –
And I wonder what it is that has left this rat,
30   Why a month of probing could not make it go again,
What it is that has disappeared …
    The bell has gone; it is time to go for lunch.
I fold the rat, replace it in its bag,
Wash from my hands the sweet
35   Smell of meat and formalin
And go and eat a meat pie afterwards.
    So, for four weeks or so, I am told
I shall continue to dissect this rat;
Like a child
40   Pulling apart a clock he cannot mend.

'Dissection' by Colin Rowbotham (1994)

>> Task 9.5

1. What aspects of his rat seem surprising to the narrator? Answer as fully as you can using short quotations within your answers.

2. How does the poet make his very big discoveries about life and death seem an ordinary part of school life?

3. In many ways 'Dissection' is very different from the extract from 'The Prelude' in Passage D. But do the two poems also have anything in common? Write a paragraph about the similarities between them. Consider:

   • ideas
   • feelings expressed
   • use of a narrator
   • rhythm, rhyme and pattern.

Passage F

1 HG Wells (1866-1946) was the son of an unsuccessful Kent tradesman. After a spell as an unqualified teacher Herbert
5 George Wells began to write novels and became one of the most respected and best-selling authors of his generation. His
10 books are still widely read and admired today. Some are science fiction stories which sound a note of warning. Others are about social issues. The Time Machine
15 (1895), from which this passage comes, was Wells's first success. The narrator of the novel tells a group of friends that he has invented a time machine which means
20 he can travel through time and investigate the destiny of the human race. He describes his discoveries.

As the columns of hail grew thinner, I saw the white figure more distinctly. It was very large, for a silver birch tree touched its shoulder. It was of white marble, in shape something like a winged sphinx, but the wings, instead of being carried vertically at the sides, were spread so that it seemed to hover. The pedestal, it appeared to me, was of bronze, and was thick with verdigris. It chanced that the face was towards me; the sightless eyes seemed to watch me; there was the faint shadow of a smile upon the lips. It was greatly weather-worn, and that imparted an unpleasant suggestion of disease. I stood looking at it for a little space – half a minute, perhaps, or half an hour. It seemed to advance

25 and to recede as the hail drove before it denser and thinner. At last I tore my eyes from it for a moment and saw that the hail curtain had worn threadbare, and that the sky was lightening with the promise of the Sun.

I looked up again at the crouching white shape, and the full temerity of my voyage
30 came suddenly upon me. What might appear when that hazy curtain was altogether withdrawn? What might not have happened to men? What if cruelty had grown into a common passion? What if in this interval the race had lost its manliness and had developed into something inhuman, unsympathetic, and overwhelmingly powerful? I might seem some old-world savage animal, only the more dreadful and disgusting
35 for our common likeness – a foul creature to be incontinently slain.

Already I saw other vast shapes – huge buildings with intricate parapets and tall columns, with a wooded hill-side dimly creeping in upon me through the lessening storm. I was seized with a panic fear. I turned frantically to the Time Machine, and strove hard to readjust it. As I did so the shafts of the sun smote through the
40 thunderstorm. The grey downpour was swept aside and vanished like the trailing garments of a ghost. Above me, in the intense blue of the summer sky, some faint

brown shreds of cloud whirled into nothingness. The great buildings about me stood out clear and distinct, shining with the wet of the thunderstorm, and picked out in white by the unmelted hailstones piled along their courses. I felt naked in a strange world. I felt as perhaps a bird may feel in the clear air, knowing the hawk wings above and will swoop. My fear grew to frenzy. I took a breathing space, set my teeth, and again grappled fiercely, wrist and knee, with the machine. It gave under my desperate onset and turned over. It struck my chin violently. One hand on the saddle, the other on the lever, I stood panting heavily in attitude to mount again.

But with this recovery of a prompt retreat my courage recovered. I looked more curiously and less fearfully at this world of the remote future. In a circular opening, high up in the wall of the nearer house I saw a group of figures clad in rich soft robes. They had seen me, and their faces were directed towards me.

Then I heard voices approaching me. Coming through the bushes by the White Sphinx were the heads and shoulders of men running. One of these emerged in a pathway leading straight to the little lawn upon which stood my machine. He was a slight creature – perhaps four feet high – clad in a purple tunic, girdled at the waist with a leather belt. Sandals or buskins – I could not clearly distinguish which – were on his feet; his legs were bare to the knees, and his head was bare. Noticing that, I noticed for the first time how warm the air was.

He struck me as being a very beautiful and graceful creature, but indescribably frail. His flushed face reminded me of the more beautiful kind of consumptive – that hectic beauty of which we used to hear so much. At the sight of him I suddenly regained confidence. I took my hands from the machine.

In another moment we were standing face to face, I and this fragile thing out of futurity. He came straight up to me and laughed into my eyes. The absence in his bearing of any sign of fear struck me at once. Then he turned to two others who were following him and spoke to them in a strange and very sweet and liquid tongue.

There were others coming, and presently a little group of perhaps eight or ten of these exquisite creatures were about me. One of them addressed me. It came into my head, oddly enough, that my voice was too harsh and deep for them. So I shook my head, and, pointing to my ears, shook it again. He came a step forward, hesitated, and then touched my hand. Then I felt other soft and little tentacles upon my shoulders and back. They wanted to make sure I was real. There was nothing in this that was at all alarming. Indeed, there was something in these pretty little people that inspired confidence – a graceful gentleness, a certain childlike ease. And besides, they looked so frail that I could fancy myself flinging the whole dozen of them about like nine-pins. But I made a sudden motion to warn them when I saw their pink little hands feeling at the Time Machine. Happily then, when it was not too late I thought of a danger I had hitherto forgotten, and reaching over the bars of the machine I unscrewed the little levers that would set it in motion, and put these in my pocket. Then I turned again to see what I could do in the way of communication.

85 And then, looking more nearly into their features, I saw some further peculiarities in their Dresden-china type of prettiness. Their hair, which was uniformly curly, came to a sharp end at the neck and cheek; there was not the faintest suggestion of it on the face, and their ears were singularly minute. The mouths were small, with bright red, rather thin lips, and the little chins ran to a point. The eyes were large and mild; and – this may seem egotism on my part – I fancied even that there was a certain lack of the interest I might have expected in them.

90 As they made no effort to communicate with me, but simply stood around me smiling and speaking in soft cooing notes to each other, I began the conversation. I pointed to the Time Machine and to myself. Then hesitating for a moment how to express time, I pointed to the sun. At once a quaintly pretty little figure in chequered purple and white followed my gesture, and then astonished me by imitating the
95 sound of thunder.

For a moment I was staggered, though the import of his gesture was plain enough. The question had come into my mind abruptly: were these creatures fools? You may hardly understand how it took me. You see I had always anticipated that the people of the year Eight Hundred and Two Thousand odd would be incredibly in front of us
100 in knowledge, art, everything. Then one of them suddenly asked me a question that showed him to be on the intellectual level of our five-year-old children – asked me, in fact, if I had come from the sun in a thunderstorm! It let loose the judgement I had suspended upon their clothes, their frail, light limbs, and fragile features. A flow of disappointment rushed across my mind. For a moment I felt I had built the Time
105 Machine in vain.

From *The Time Machine* by HG Wells (1895)

>> Task 9.6

1   Describe the 'exquisite' creatures in your own words. What disappoints the narrator about them?

2.   Why is it appropriate for this extract to be included in a chapter whose theme is discovery? Answer in as much detail as you can.

3.   The traveller is in 'the remote future' (line 51) at this point in the novel. Had you not known that would you have thought he had moved forwards or backwards in time? Give reasons for your answer and back it up with close reference to the passage.

Writing about literature

Study this example of how you might write in detail about these two lines from 'Dissection':

> Fingering the damp, yellow fur, I know
> That this first touch is far the worst.

Rowbotham's decision to open this sentence with a fronted phrase means that he can emphasise the word 'fingering' with its repellent connotations of touching something implicitly revolting. The simple adjectives 'damp' and 'yellow' reinforce his repugnance as the narrator tries to do to the rat what he has to do. Half way through the sentence comes the subject 'I' and the statement that 'this first touch is far the worst'. Apart from the almost onomatopoeically slow three-syllable word 'fingering', and the long vowelled 'yellow', the entire sentence is monosyllabic. It is the basic language that a school student would use to his or her friends so it seems very natural. It also strengthens the effect of what he is saying to use straightforward language rather than clutter his thoughts up with longer words derived from Latin. Each of the short words here has an impact of its own like a little hammer blow. All the dread which he has been feeling for some time about this moment is communicated.

>> Task 9.7

Choose two to four lines from one or other of the poems in this chapter. Write a detailed analysis of them, modelled on the above example.

Personal Writing

>> Task 9.8

1. Write about an important time in your life – or event or discovery – in the form of a poem like the extract from 'The Prelude'. It need not rhyme. (The technical name for unrhymed poetry is blank verse.) But try to make your lines even by using the same number of syllables that Wordsworth does.

---

2. Write a short story called 'The Time Machine' or, if you have not read HG Wells's novel, write a continuation of the passage above.

---

3. Write a short biographical essay – using the style of the *Oxford Dictionary of National Biography* – about a well-known person who has recently died. You may be able to get your information from obituaries, especially if you collect them from several different newspapers. You can almost always access obituaries through newspapers' websites too.

4. Write a piece about Alexander Fleming suitable for inclusion in a children's book. Base it on the information in Passage A. Decide what age your readers are before you start.

5. Write about something you have learned or discovered in school as Colin Rowbotham does. It can be a personal account or a poem.

6. Write about discovery in any way you wish.

Writing tip

It is not usually good style to clutter up your writing with too many adjectives and adverbs. Instead choose strong and appropriate verbs and nouns. Use adverbs and adjectives only if they are really necessary or add something.

For example:

> 'The water gushed along the gully' is a much better sentence than 'A huge amount of water ran quickly along the bottom of the steep little valley'.

> 'Palaeontologists have discovered the remains of a dinosaur in a desert in China' is a much better sentence than 'Fossil experts have discovered the preserved body of a prehistoric animal in a lonely, dry place in China'.

Using strong verbs and nouns will usually help you to create shorter sentences (see above) too.

If you feel tempted to use the adverb 'actually', or the adjective 'actual', ask yourself if you really need it. Try your sentence without it. You may be surprised how well it works when it is free of these 'clutter words'. Other examples include: extremely, very, only, indeed.

WORD BANK

Eve Curie used a **pseudonym – a pen** or **false name**. It comes from the Ancient Greek *pseudes* (false) and *onoma* (name).

You can make it into an adjective (The author decided to be pseudonymous), an adverb (She wrote pseudonymously) or another noun (She decided on psuedonymity).

We get a number of English words from *onoma*.

>> Task 9.9

Write a definition of each of the following words and give examples of each. You can use the adjectival, adverbial or other noun form if you wish:

1. homonym
2. toponym
3. synonym
4. eponym

5. antonym
6. acronym
7. metonym
8. cryptonym

Alexander Fleming's work led to the development of antibiotics and work on antiseptic and antibacterial treatments. The prefix **anti**- comes from the Ancient Greek word *anti* – meaning **against**. Think of words such as anticlimax and anticlockwise.

Words starting with anti often need a hyphen because the two halves of the word have been put together fairly recently. And you can make them up. Consider: anti-school, anti-government, anti-sports, anti-hunting and so on.

Another group of words starts with **ante**- (or shortened forms of it) from the Ancient Greek *ante* – meaning **before**. Think of antenatal classes which are held for parents before the birth of their baby. Ancestor, anticipate and antique all include shortened forms of ante-.

>> Task 9.10

Use the following words derived from *anti* and *ante* to show you understand their meaning:

1. anterior
2. antisocial
3. antifreeze
4. antepenultimate

5. anteroom
6. anti-nuclear
7. antedate
8. antebellum

> **>> Task 9.11**
>
> Work with a partner. Each of you should skim the passages in this chapter for ten words which he or she thinks the other might not be able to spell. Give your list to your partner and agree a time for learning the spellings on the list – perhaps 15 minutes. Then test each other. Relearn any you each got wrong. Then swap lists and try it the other way round.
>
> Note: it isn't very useful to be able to spell words aloud and can be quite difficult. Many of us learn to spell partly from the visual 'shape' of a word. It is far more important to be able to write words accurately. So when you are testing a partner he or she should always write the words. It helps most people to write them for practice during the learning process too.

NUTS AND BOLTS

In English lessons – and later at university or work – you are often asked, or need, to summarise something you have read. I've asked you to do it in various forms many times in this book. Expressing information in a shorter form used to be called writing a précis and was a formal task often set in English examinations in the past. It is still a very valuable skill.

In order to extract the essence of a piece of writing:

- skim-read it

- then read it properly at least twice

- aim to reduce it to a third or less of its length

- use your own words in the summary/précis rather than 'lifting' shortened chunks from the original

- use general or collective terms to sum up. For example, if the writer mentions cups, a kettle, spoons, ladles and a food mixer in a description of a kitchen you might call these 'kitchen utensils' (or 'tools' or 'equipment'). If a writer mentions Dickens, Trollope, Charlotte Brontë and Wilkie Collins you might refer to them in your summary as Victorian novelists.

- remember what we learned in Chapters 7 and 8 about dependent or subordinate phrases. The information in these can usually be discarded in summary. Look for the main clause in the sentence for the central point the writer is making.

- make judgements about which information really matters and which can be discarded.

Study this example, taken from a study guide by Susan Elkin on *To Kill a Mockingbird* by Harper Lee (published by Philip Allan Updates, 2005):

> Harper Lee was born in Monroeville, Alabama, in 1926. She was the youngest of three children and her father was a lawyer.

Jean Louise ('Scout') Finch, the narrator of *To Kill a Mockingbird* was born in the same year as her creator in a fictional Alabama town called Maycomb. Scout's father, Atticus, is a lawyer and she is the younger child in the family.

To Kill a Mockingbird is a good example of fiction that has developed from the author's personal experiences. Maycomb is based on Monroeville and Atticus is based on Harper Lee's own father. (97 words)

Here is the same information summarised:

In her partly autobiographical novel, Harper Lee creates a fictional version of her Alabama home town, a narrator who is a self-portrait and a character, Atticus, modelled on her lawyer father. (31 words)

The essential information is still there but the length is reduced by two thirds.

▸▸ Task 9.12

Summarise this passage entitled 'Respecting Earthworms', which was also written by Susan Elkin for *Country-Side*, the magazine of the British Naturalists Association, Spring 2007. It has 121 words. Reduce it to about 40.

Note: this piece is written in the first person – the author uses her own 'I' voice. When you summarise, give an account of what she says in the third person. Do not write as if you were her. You will probably need to write 'The author …'

Like every other child almost everywhere, I'd watched earthworms – pink, brown, long, short, fat, thin – wriggling about in the garden from babyhood. A reasonably observant child, I'd noticed that they have segments and that about a third of the way down their length there is a thick shiny 'saddle'. And my green-fingered grandfather had taught me that earthworms are nature's gardeners and must therefore be respected.

But it wasn't until, aged 16, in one of my very first A level zoology practical lessons, that I became intimately acquainted with *Lumbricus terrestris*. This particular specimen lay under water in a flat pan having been drowned for my education. My task was to dissect it. And what a lot I learned.

Practice is a noun:

- I must do some trumpet practice.
- Practice is important if you want to improve your badminton.
- Dr Singh's medical practice covered three villages.

Sometimes it becomes an adjective:

- Practice tapes are useful for French oral work.
- The hour before supper is practice time for tennis.

Practise is a verb:

- I must practise the trumpet.
- Practise your badminton if you want to improve.
- Dr Singh practises in three villages.

Use **advice** and **advise** to help you remember this 'c or s rule' for nouns and verbs. They are easier because they sound different. Say aloud:

- Please give me your advice. (noun)
- We could try the advice centre. (adjective)
- I advise you to apologise. (verb)
- She advised me to come. (verb)

Licence/license and **prophecy/prophesy** follow the same pattern.

Be aware that you may see this 'wrong' in American writing. In American English these words are always spelled with a 'c' even when they are verbs.

More speaking and listening activities

Suppose you could travel in HG Wells's Time Machine. Tell a partner 'where' (should that be 'when'?) you would like to go in it and why.

Discuss in small groups whether or not you think it is right to dissect dead animals for education and learning as the narrator of Colin Rowbotham's poem does.

Which scientific (or other) discovery do you think has made the most difference to the development of the human race? Work out your views by talking it over with a partner or in a small group. Then organise a whole class discussion in which you try to persuade others to your way of thinking.

Research the work of a great scientist such as Alexander Fleming or Marie Curie – and there are plenty of others to choose from. Organise your findings into a two-minute presentation for the rest of the class.

With your teacher's agreement invite an outside speaker – who has made some kind of discovery – to talk to your class or to the school. It could, for example, be someone who has researched some aspect of local history or conducted a survey in your area.

Palindromes

Words such as **eve**, **refer** and **minim** are known as palindromes because their letters are the same whether you read them forwards or backwards. The word **palindrome** comes from the Greek *palindromos* which means **running back again**.

So a palindrome is a word, phrase, sentence, poem or whatever which reads the same backwards as it does forward.

In the case of a word, phrase or short sentence (level, noon, madam) it's a question of the order of the letters.

Consider this sentence which comes from James Joyce's novel *Ulysses* (1922): Able was I ere I saw Elba.

Or this anonymous one: Marge lets Norah see Sharon's telegram.

You can also make palindromic sentences by ordering whole words rather than letters.

For example: You hit Ali before Ali hit you.

Or here's a famous line from Alexander Dumas's novel *The Three Musketeers* (1844): All for one and one for all.

Palindromic dates are fun too. 9th November 1990 could be written 09.11.90 for example. Or 1st November 2010 will be 01.11.10.

- Think of some more palindromic words (include proper nouns such as Otto)

- Identify other palindromic dates

- Invent some palindromic sentences.

WIDE RANGE READING

Rare Treasures: Mary Anning and her Remarkable Discoveries by Don Brown (2003). Mary Anning was a Dorset-based Victorian lady. When people began to realise the scientific significance of fossils Miss Anning became deeply interested. So she went out to the local rocks with her hammer and studied what she found. Soon she was one of the country's foremost palaeontologists with many discoveries to her name. A large section at the Natural History Museum in London is devoted to Mary Anning and her important work – very unusual for a woman in her day. She had to remain an 'amateur' because 'real' scientists in universities were, of course, all men.

Dissolution by CJ Sansom (2003). All detective novels are about discovery and this one's a real cracker. Matthew Shardlake is a lawyer in Henry VIII's England. The monasteries are being dismantled but, in one of them, there are mysterious murders which Shardlake has to investigate. There are some wonderful characters in this novel such as Guy the black monk. The Tudor background is beautifully done – lots of smells, sights and atmosphere. If you enjoy this exciting page-turner as much as I did, there are three other (so far) Shardlake novels for you to move on to.

Pastwatch: the Redemption of Christopher Columbus by Orson Scott Card (1996). Known as Cristóbal Colón in Spanish, Columbus (1451–1506) was an Italian navigator who worked for the Portuguese government. He sailed to what we now call America four times and, for hundreds of years, was credited with being the first European to reach it in 1492. It is now known that the Vikings 'discovered' Canada and north America centuries earlier. This is an interesting book about Columbus's achievements which makes you think about what we mean by 'discovery'. After all, the native Americans (now known as American Indians or Amerindians) had been there for thousands of years.

The Tomb of Tutenkhamun by Howard Carter and AC Mace (2008). People had been searching for the lost tomb of the Ancient Egyptian 'boy king' Tutenkhamun for decades. Finally, in 1922, after years of trying, Howard Carter found it in the Valley of the Kings near Luxor in Egypt – complete with the treasures which had been buried with the King. Quite a discovery. This new book, published to coincide with some of the treasure being put on temporary display in London at the time, is the late Mr Carter's own fascinating account of what happened then and afterwards – edited and added to by A C Mace.

David Livingstone by Rob Mackenzie (2000). David Livingstone (1813–1873) was a Scottish missionary explorer who worked in Africa. He was the first European to follow the Zambezi River to its mouth and the first to see Victoria Falls – hailed as a great discovery. He mapped a lot of Africa for the first time and helped to stop the Arab slave trade. This biography brings Livingstone's achievements and discoveries to life – and makes us understand just how hard the work must have been, especially for his wife who travelled with him.

The White Darkness by Geraldine McCaughrean (2005). This is an entertaining novel narrated by a teenage girl who is 'in love' with Captain Oates, one of the men who accompanied Robert Falcon Scott on his fatal attempt to be the first to reach the South Pole in 1911. Scott, Oates and the others were beaten to the Pole by a Norwegian team. They all died. We know what happened from Scott's journals which were found the following spring. The brave Oates was one of the first to die because he took himself off into the cold night alone to save the others having to look after him. This novel, intended for young readers, includes a modern – very strange – trip to Antarctica.

MOVING ON

- Find your way round the (very useful) *Oxford Dictionary of National Biography* by looking up the entries for HG Wells and William Wordsworth. Then think of two or three more people whose lives interest you and look them up too. (Note: to be included in the ODNB a person must be (a) British and (b) dead!)

- Alexander Fleming and the Curies all won Nobel prizes. So did HG Wells. Find out about Alfred Nobel and the prizes named after him. Study the lists of prize winners for the various categories over the years. Prepare a short presentation on this subject for the rest of the class.

- Imagine you had been asked to choose the extracts for this chapter. Your brief is to find five or six passages of fiction, poetry, non-fiction, opinion, memoirs – or anything else you wish – which fits the theme with as much variety as possible.

READY FOR A REAL CHALLENGE?

Make a study of the life and times of William Wordsworth. Read a biography of William Wordsworth such as *William Wordsworth: a Biography* by Hunter Davis (Sutton Publishing, 1997) or *William Wordsworth: a Life* by Stephen Gill (Oxford paperbacks, 2000). Then read *The Prelude*. Wordsworth's sister, Dorothy, who was very close to her brother, also wrote journals which are interesting to read and compare.

Who would you say is the most evil person you have ever heard of – in real life in the past or present or in fiction? What makes a person evil? Think of a few names you would certainly have on your list. What do they have in common?

This chapter's title comes from Shakespeare's play *Richard III*. At the beginning of the play the Duke of Gloucester, soon to be the eponymous (look it up if necessary!) King Richard, reveals his 'subtle, false and treacherous' intentions to the audience.

In the passages which open this chapter we meet – through different sorts of writing – various people who are subtle, false or treacherous (or all three) ranging from the fictional Sweeney Todd, who was the subject of a 2008 film, to two very different characters from 19th century novels and two very real monsters from the past, King Leopold of Belgium and Adolf Hitler. Then there's a poem about another sort of villain.

Passage A

1

Sweeney Todd is a legend - the story of a London barber who was also a serial murderer. No one is quite sure whether

5

there are any nuggets of truth underlying the legend but writers - and musicians in the case of Stephen Sondheim - have often been creative with it. Here a

10

journalist reviews the 2008 film of Sondheim's musical. Note what a lot you learn about the story and the film from the writer's reactions to it even if you

15

haven't seen the film yourself.

Sweeney Todd: The Demon Barber of Fleet Street
Certificate 18, 116 mins
Stars: Johnny Depp, Helena Bonham Carter, Alan Rickman, Timothy Spall, Sacha Baron Cohen, Edward Sanders, Jayne Wisener, Jamie Campbell Bower
Directed by Tim Burton

A ghoulishly compelling Victorian horror story, and a film director with an unrepentant gothic passion for the macabre may sound like a marriage made in heaven (or hell). But what happens when the issue of that fiendish union is a musical?

20

But *Sweeney Todd: The Demon Barber of Fleet Street* is not your average musical. And Tim Burton is not your average filmmaker.

Based on Stephen Sondheim's award-winning 1979 musical of the same name, Burton takes Sondheim's magnificently eclectic, bitingly satirical score and uses it to bring to life a terrible and bloody tale of corruption, crushed innocence, insanity, serial murder and cannibalism.

25 And he does so with a spectacular visual flair, buckets of blood and a deliciously wicked sense of the blackest gallows humour.

Many will be familiar with the infamous 18th century exploits of Sweeney Todd – the so-called Demon Barber – who gave a whole new meaning to a close shave with an extremely sharp cut-throat razor and his enterprising landlady who served his
30 unfortunate customers up as pies in her shop.

But Burton has a soft spot for a certain type of monster. Instead of the gruesome exploits of a pair of avaricious murderers he gives us a very human tragedy of lost love and the devastating consequences of obsessive revenge.

The bombast and sheer theatricality of Sondheim's songs remain, but in using actors
35 who can sing rather than singers who act, the emphasis here is on dramatic performance and story rather than song. This is further ensured by paring down the musical numbers to their most basic and potent elements – there are no singing crowds, or OTT choral refrains. The songs are worked into the drama, it doesn't stop for them.

40 An excellent cast includes: Johnny Depp, Helena Bonham Carter, Alan Rickman, Timothy Spall and Sacha Baron Cohen.

Benjamin Barker (Depp) is an honest barber happily married to the beautiful Lucy (Laura Michelle Kelly). They live a happy, simple life with their baby daughter until they are torn apart by the depraved lust of the rich and powerful Judge Turpin
45 (Rickman), who has designs on Lucy.

Barker is arrested on a trumped-up charge and summarily deported to Australia.

Escaping 15-years later, Barker returns to London as Sweeney Todd, a shadow of his former self, to discover that his family is gone. His loyal landlady Mrs Lovett (Bonham Carter) returns his precious razors, which she has devotedly guarded, with
50 the devastating news that Lucy poisoned herself after a horrific encounter with the judge and his depraved friends. His now grown-up daughter Johanna (Wisener) is the unwilling ward of the corrupt Turpin, who lusts after her as he once lusted after her mother.

Consumed by rage, Sweeney swears vengeance, and woe betide any who cross his path.

55 *Sweeney Todd: The Demon Barber of Fleet Street* will not be to everyone's taste. Anyone who has seen Burton's *Sleepy Hollow* will have an idea what to expect. This is a darkly macabre film; the combination of beautifully orchestral song and the literal explosions of arterial blood from slashed throats is truly disturbing and often alarmingly comic.

Johnny Depp as Sweeney Todd with Alan Rickman

60 Production designer Dante Ferretti and director of photography Dariusz Wolski have created a wonderful, highly stylised gothic cityscape full of filthy claustrophobic streets, impossibly angled rooms, yawning sewers and terrifyingly threatening everyday appliances. London through Sweeney's eyes is a vice ridden pit where those in power take pleasure in destroying those without any.

65 The almost monochromatic palette of blacks and greys, make the sudden splashes of scarlet blood all the more shocking and make colourful scenes of the happier past look all the more jarring. It also gives a bizarre dreamlike quality to Mrs Lovett's blue-skied fantasies of an imagined blissful future.

Costume designer Colleen Atwood kits out the cast in a fabulous variety of gothic
70 grandeur which along with corpse-pale, hollow-eyed complexions and a series of amazingly outrageous hairstyles make the Adams family look positively mundane.

The only spots of light are those lucky enough not to have yet been corrupted. Johanna (Wisener) and her young protector Anthony (Jamie Campbell Bower) can only escape by literally trying to escape from London before it is too late.

75 The gory heart of the proceedings is Johnny Depp who excels as the homicidally driven Todd. His consuming obsession for revenge puts him on a tragic path that

annihilates everything he was and any future he may have. So enmeshed is he with death he is no longer truly alive. Depp sings the role with a surprisingly good voice, bringing a melodic hard edge that spookily imitates David Bowie at times.

80 He is ably supported by Bonham Carter who is excellent as the amoral yet oddly sweet Mrs Lovett, who daydreams of a lovely life by the sea with Sweeney as she happily prepares her latest batch of pies with her innocent adopted street urchin, Toby (an angelically voiced Edward Sanders), blissfully ignorant of their special ingredients.

85 Alan Rickman is creepily evil as Turpin, the seemingly pious judge who takes perverse delight in abusing his power, although he is sadly, a little underused. Timothy Spall is truly repellent as his oily, sadistic side-kick, Beadle Bamford. Sacha Baron Cohen is flamboyantly pompous as the boastful Adolfo Pirelli, who comes to a sticky end after trying to blackmail Sweeney.

90 This is a bloody, brilliant, cautionary tale of a good man who gives himself so totally over to his dark side's raging hate, that it eventually consumes him too.

By Gail Campbell Thomson, *Liverpool Daily Post*, 25th January 2008

>> Task 10.1

1. Summarise the story of Sweeney Todd in your own words.

2. What particularly impressed the writer about the film? Answer in as much detail as you can.

3. What warnings does the writer give about the film?

4. Would you go and see this film on the strength of this review? Explain your answer?

10 Subtle, False and Treacherous English Year 9

Passage B

Adolf Hitler became Chancellor of Germany in 1933. Popular with some at first, Hitler quickly became a ruthless leader under whose government Jews and others were ruthlessly persecuted. By the end of the Second World War (1939-1945) six million people had died in death camps. This extract comes from a speech given by Hitler at the Reichstag (German Parliament) on 13th July 1934 two weeks after more than 100 people had been killed on 30 June - an event known as The Night of the Long Knives. Look carefully at what he says, translated into English from German. Remember that he had been Chancellor for only a year. The events of the war were still in the future.

At one o'clock in the night I received the last dispatches telling me of the alarm summonses; at two o'clock in the morning I flew to Munich. Meanwhile Minister-President Göring had previously received from me the commission that if I proceeded to apply a purge he was to take similar measures at once in Berlin and in Prussia. With an iron fist he beat down the attack on the National Socialist state before it could develop. The necessity for acting with lightening speed meant that in this decisive hour I had very few men with me. In the presence of Minister Goebbels and of the new Chief of Staff the action of which you are already informed was executed and brought to a close in Munich. Although only a few days before I had been prepared to exercise clemency, at this hour there was no place for any such consideration. Mutinies are suppressed in accordance with laws of iron that are eternally the same. If anyone reproaches me and asks why I did not resort to the regular courts of justice for conviction of the offenders, then all I can say to him is this: in this hour I was responsible for the fate of the German people, and thereby I became the supreme justiciar of the German people!

Mutinous divisions have in all periods been recalled to order by decimation. Only one state has failed to make use of its articles of war, and this state paid for that failure by collapse – Germany. I did not wish to deliver up the young Reich to the fate of the old Reich. I gave the order to shoot those who were the ringleaders in this treason, and I further gave the order to burn out down to the raw flesh the ulcers of this poisoning of the wells in our domestic life and of the poisoning of the outside world. And I further ordered that if any of the mutineers should attempt to resist arrest, they were immediately to be struck down with armed force. The nation must know that its existence – and that is guaranteed through its internal order and security – can be threatened by no one with impunity! And everyone must know that for all

192

future time that if he raises his hand to strike the state, then certain death is his
45　lot. And every National Socialist must know that no rank or position can protect him from his personal responsibility and therefore from his punishment. I have prosecuted
50　thousands of our former opponents on account of their corruption. I should in my own mind reproach myself if I were now to tolerate similar offences in our own ranks. No people and no
55　government can help it if creatures arise such as we once knew in Germany, a Kutisker, for example, such as France came to know in a Stavisky, or such as we have today once more experienced –
60　men whose aim it is to sin against a nation's interests. But every people is itself guilty if it does not find the strength to destroy such creatures.

If people bring against me the objection that only a judicial procedure could precisely
65　weigh the measure of the guilt and of its expiation, then against this view I lodge my most solemn protest. He who rises against Germany is a traitor to his country: and the traitor to his country is not to be punished according to the range and the extent of his act, but according to the purpose that that act has revealed. He who has in his heart purposes to raise a mutiny and thereby breaks loyalty, breaks faith, breaks sacred
70　pledges, he can expect nothing else than that he himself will be the first sacrifice. I have no intention to have the little culprits shot and to spare the great criminals. It is not my duty to enquire whether it was too hard a lot that was inflicted upon these conspirators, these agitators and destroyers, these poisoners of the wellsprings of German public opinion: it is not mine to consider which of them suffered too severely:
75　I have only to see to it that Germany's lot should not be intolerable.

From a speech given by Adolf Hitler at the Reichstag, 13th July 1934.

>> Task 10.2

1. Summarise what happened on The Night of the Long Knives.

2. How does Hitler explain or excuse his decision not to use normal legal procedures to deal with the alleged traitors?

3. What evidence can you find in this passage to show that Hitler was already a ruthless man five years before the outbreak of the Second World War?

4. What arguments does he use to persuade his listeners that he is trustworthy and made the right decisions?

Passage C

1
By the late 1860s every European country which wanted them had valuable colonies in Africa and elsewhere. King Leopold II of

5
Belgium (1835-1909) thought Belgium had missed out. So he took Congo Free State* and exploited it ruthlessly to make a huge fortune from ivory and other products. His

10
main agent in the Congo was Henry Stanley, an American journalist. Another (modern) American Journalist, Adam Hochschild, gives a horrifying account of what Leopold and Stanley did in his book King Leopold's Ghost: A Story of Greed,

15
Terror and Heroism in Colonial Africa. For decades Stanley was regarded as a great

20
hero. Hochschild's thorough and skilled investigative journalism shows Stanley in his true colours.

They agreed that Stanley would first set up a base near the river's mouth and then construct a road around the rapids, through the rugged Crystal Mountains – a precursor to a railway. Over this road porters would carry several steamboats broken down into small pieces, which Stanley would later assemble and use to travel upstream, building a chain of trading stations along the thousand-mile navigable main stretch of the Congo River. Afterward he would write a book about his experiences – but Leopold would have the right to edit it.

Of the riches Leopold hoped to find in the Congo, the one that gleamed most brightly in his imagination was ivory. European and American

* Now Democratic Republic of Congo, previously Zaire from 1971 to 1997.

25   merchants were already eagerly buying African ivory in the markets of Zanzibar.
Because it could be easily carved, ivory in the nineteenth century was a more rare
and expensive version of what plastic is today, with the added cachet of having an
exotic origin – a cachet that grew greater with the public idolisation of African
explorers. Ivory from elephant tusks was shaped into knife handles, billiard balls,
30   combs, fans, napkin rings, piano and organ keys, chess pieces, crucifixes, snuffboxes,
brooches, and statuettes. In a faint echo of its original use to the elephant, it was
made into false teeth. Despite the long distances the ivory had to be carried from the
elephant ranges far inland, it was attractive to dealers all the way along the line
because, like drugs or precious metals, it had high value and low bulk. The hundred
35   pounds of ivory in an average pair of African elephant tusks could make hundreds of
piano keys or thousands of false teeth. Ivory dealers preferred African elephants to
Indian, and the elephants of equatorial Africa, which included the Congo basin,
tended to have the largest tusks of all. Stanley had found ivory so plentiful that it
was used for doorposts in African homes.

40   For the moment, such riches lay at least several years in Leopold's future, for first
Stanley had to build his road. He left nothing out of the detailed budget he
prepared for the king: small boats, wooden buildings in pieces, rope, tools, African
porters, and European supervisors. Among the latter were two young Englishmen
who, in the tradition of Stanley's inept subordinates, had never been out of the
45   country. Having hired neophytes, he could rail about their inexperience: 'I have no
friend on any expedition, no one who could possibly be my companion, on an
equal footing, except while with Livingstone … How can he who has witnessed
many wars hope to be understood by one whose most shocking sight has been a
nose-bleed?'

50   Stanley was savvy enough to demand his money from Leopold in advance because,
despite a plethora of contracts, whom he was working for remained foggy: was it
the king himself, the king's International African Association, which seemed to be
withering away, or a new and somewhat secretive body called the Committee for
Studies of the Upper Congo? The committee's stockholders officially were a small
55   group of Dutch and British businessmen and a Belgian banker – who, in fact, was
quietly holding a large block of shares as Leopold's proxy. A trusted henchman of the
king's, Colonel Maximilien Strauch, was the committee's president.

Ambitious as his and Stanley's plans were, Leopold was intent that they be seen as
nothing more than philanthropy. The contracts Stanley made his European staff sign
60   forbade them to divulge anything about the real purposes of their work. 'Only
scientific explorations are intended', Leopold assured a journalist. To anyone who
questioned further he could point to a clause in the committee's charter which
explicitly prohibited it from pursuing political ends. The king wanted to protect
himself against the widespread feeling in Belgium that, for a small country, a colony

65 would be a money-losing extravagance. He also wanted to do nothing to alert any potential rivals for this appetising slice of the African cake, especially France, which was starting to show interest.

From *King Leopold's Ghost* by Adam Hochschild (1998)

➤➤ Task 10.3

1. Summarise Stanley's job in the Congo.

2. What steps did Leopold take to conceal his real purpose?

3. From the way he presents Stanley and Leopold and describes their activities and attitudes what do you think Hochschild's view is? Look carefully at vocabulary especially words such as 'savvy', 'assured', 'ambitious' and 'quietly'.

Passage D

1

In Emily Brontë's famous novel, Lockwood, the narrator visits Wuthering Heights (uninvited) for the first time. He meets the

5

house's owner, Heathcliff, who is not exactly welcoming. Notice how Brontë creates a sinister, uneasy atmosphere in which neither

10

narrator nor reader is ever quite sure what is going on. We are immediately interested in the enigmatic Heathcliff but it is clear that we shouldn't trust him.

I took a seat at the end of the hearthstone opposite that towards which my landlord advanced, and filled up an interval of silence by attempting to caress the canine mother, who had left her nursery, and was sneaking wolfishly to the back of my leg, her lip curled up, and her white teeth watering for snatch.

My caress provoked a long, guttural snarl.

15 'You'd better let the dog alone', growled Mr Heathcliff, in unison, checking fiercer demonstrations with a punch of his foot. 'She's not accustomed to be spoiled – not kept for a pet.'

Then, striding to a side door, he shouted again.

'Joseph!'

20   Joseph mumbled indistinctly in the depths of the cellar, but gave no intimation of ascending; so his master dived down to him, leaving me vis-à-vis the ruffianly bitch, and a pair of grim shaggy sheep dogs, who shared with her a jealous guardianship over all my movements.

Not anxious to come in contact with their fangs, I sat still; but imagining they would
25   scarcely understand tacit insults, I unfortunately indulged in winking and making faces at the trio, and some turn of my physiognomy so irritated madam, that she suddenly broke into a fury and leapt on my knees. I flung her back, and hastened to interpose the table between us. This proceeding aroused the whole hive. Half-a-dozen four-footed fiends of various sizes and ages, issued from hidden dens to the
30   common centre. I felt my heels and coat-laps peculiar subjects of assault; and, parrying off the larger combatants with the poker, I was constrained to demand, aloud, assistance from some of the household, in re-establishing peace.

Mr Heathcliff and his man climbed the cellar steps with vexatious phlegm. I don't think they moved one second faster than usual, though the hearth was an absolute
35   tempest of worrying and yelping.

Happily, an inhabitant of the kitchen made more dispatch; a lusty dame, with tucked up gown, bare arms, and fire-flushed cheeks, rushed into the midst of us flourishing a frying-pan; and used that weapon, and her tongue, to such purpose, that the storm subsided magically, and she only remained, heaving like a sea after a high wind,
40   when her master entered on the scene.

'What the devil is the matter?' he asked, eying me in a manner I could ill endure after this inhospitable treatment.

'What the devil indeed!' I muttered. 'The herd of possessed swine could have no worse spirits in them than those animals of yours, sir. You might as well leave a
45   stranger with a brood of tigers!'

'They won't meddle with persons who touch nothing', he remarked, putting the bottle before me, and restoring the displaced table. 'The dogs do right to be vigilant. Take a glass of wine?'

'No, thank you.'

50   'Not bitten are you?'

'If I had been, I would have set my signet on the biter.'

Heathcliff's countenance relaxed into a grin.

'Come, come', he said, 'you are flurried, Mr Lockwood. Here, take a little wine. Guests are so exceedingly rare in this house that I and my dogs, I am willing to own,
55 hardly know how to receive them. Your health, sir.'

I bowed and returned the pledge, beginning to perceive that it would be foolish to sit sulking for the misbehaviour of a pack of curs; besides I felt loath to yield the fellow further amusement, at my expense; since his humour took that turn.

He – probably swayed by prudential considerations of the folly of offending a good
60 tenant – relaxed, a little, in the laconic style of chipping off his pronouns, and auxiliary verbs; and introduced what he supposed would be a subject of interest to me, a discourse on the advantages and disadvantages of my present place of retirement.

I found him very intelligent on the topics we touched; and before I went home, I was
65 encouraged so far as to volunteer another visit, to-morrow.

He evidently wished no repetition of my intrusion. I shall go, notwithstanding. It is astonishing how sociable I feel myself compared with him.

From *Wuthering Heights* by Emily Brontë (1848)

▸▸ Task 10.4

What impression do you get of Heathcliff from this passage? Answer in as much detail as you can weaving short quotations (using inverted commas) into your sentences. Look carefully at what Heathcliff says and does. Think, too, about what the author is using the dogs to tell you.

Passage D

1 In this passage Tom, the boy at the centre of The Water Babies, first meets the bullying Grimes who will be his master.

5 Tom will work for Grimes as a boy chimney sweep climbing up and sweeping chimneys in big houses that are too narrow for an adult to get through. Like many bullies, Grimes is easily intimidated

10 by others with greater strength or authority as this extract shows. The Water Babies (1863) helped to make the public more aware of the dangers of

15 boys working as chimney sweepers which finally became illegal in 1875.

A wicket in the door opened, and out looked a tremendous old brass blunderbuss charged up to the muzzle with slugs, who was the porter; and Tom started back at the sight of him.

'What case is this?' he asked in a deep voice; out of his broad bell mouth.

'If you please, sir it is no case; only a young gentleman from her ladyship, who wants to see Grimes, the master-sweep.'

'Grimes?' said the blunderbuss. And he pulled in his muzzle, perhaps to look over his prison-lists.

'Grimes is up chimney No 345', he said from the inside. 'So the young gentleman had better go on to the roof.'

20 Tom looked up at the enormous wall, which seemed at least ninety miles high, and wondered how he should ever get up: but when he hinted that to the truncheon, it settled the matter in a moment. For it whisked round and gave him a shove behind as sent him up to the roof in no time, with his little dog under his arm.

And there he walked along the leads, till he met another truncheon, and told him
25 his errand.

'Very good', it said. Come along: but it will be no use. He is the most unremorseful, hard-hearted, foul-mouthed fellow I have in charge; and thinks about nothing but beer and pipes; which are not allowed here, of course.

So they walked along over the leads, and very sooty they were, and Tom thought the
30 chimneys must want sweeping very much. But he was surprised to see that the soot did not stick to his feet, or dirty them in the least.

And at last they came to chimney No 345. Out of the top of it, his head and shoulders just showing, stuck poor Mr Grimes, so sooty, and bleared, and ugly, that Tom could hardly bear to look at him. And in his mouth was a pipe; but it was not
35 alight; though he was pulling at it with all his might.

'Attention, Mr Grimes', said the truncheon; 'here is a gentleman come to see you.'

But Grimes only said bad words; and kept grumbling. 'My pipe won't draw. My pipe won't draw.'

40 'Keep a civil tongue, and attend!' said the truncheon; and popped up just like Punch, hitting Grimes such a crack over the head with itself, that his brains rattled inside like a dried walnut in its shell. He tried to get his hands out, and rub the place; but he could not, for they were stuck fast in the chimney. Now he was forced to attend.

'Hey!' he said, 'why, it's Tom! I suppose you have come here to laugh at me, you spiteful little atomy?'

45 Tom assured him that he had not, but only wanted to help him.

'I don't want anything except beer, and that I can't get; and a light to this bothering pipe, and that I can't get either.'

'I'll get you one', said Tom; and he took up a live coal (there were plenty lying about) and put it to Grimes' pipe: but it went out instantly.

50 'It's no use' said the truncheon, leaning itself against the chimney and looking on. 'I tell you, it is no use. His heart is so cold that it freezes everything that comes near him. You will see that presently, plain enough.'

'Oh, of course, it's my fault. Everything's always my fault', said Grimes. 'Now don't go to hit me again' (for the truncheon started to upright, and looked very wicked) 'you
55 know if my arms were only free you daren't hit me then'.

The truncheon leaned back against the chimney, and took no notice of the personal insult, like a well-trained policeman as it was, though he was ready enough to avenge any transgression against morality or order.

From *The Water Babies* by Charles Kingsley (1863)

›› Task 10.5

1a. What does the writer mean by the blunderbuss and the truncheon?

 b. How effective do you find these metonyms? Answer in as much detail as you can.

2. Write about the humour in this passage.

- Do you find it funny?
- Do you think it is meant to be funny?
- Write as fully as you can with short 'woven in' quotations put in inverted commas.

3. Which passage do you find the more interesting – this or Passage C? Give detailed reasons for your answer.

Passage E

Robert Browning (1812-1889) published this poem in 1836 so this gruesome narrative by a murderer is a young man's work. Notice how he describes Porphyria's beauty and innocence and contrasts with her subtle false and treacherous lover. Do you, in fact, agree with that description of him? Before you try to write about this poem discuss with a partner whether or not you think that Browning really helps us to understand the lover/murderer's feelings by presenting the poem from his point of view.

Porphyria's Lover

1 The rain set early in tonight,
        The sullen wind was soon awake,
    It tore the elm-tops down for spite,
        And did its worst to vex the lake:
5   I listened with heart fit to break
    When glided in Porphyria; straight
        She shut the cold out and the storm,
    And kneeled and made the cheerless grate
        Blaze up, and all the cottage warm;
10   Which done, she rose, and from her form
    Withdrew the dripping cloak and shawl,
        And laid her soiled gloves by, untied
    Her hat and let the damp hair fall,
        And, last, she sat down by my side
15   And called me. When no voice replied,
    She put my arm about her waist,
        And made her smooth white shoulder bare,
    And all her yellow hair displaced,
        And, stooping, made my cheek lie there,
20   And spread, o'er all, her yellow hair,
    Murmuring how she loved me—she
        Too weak, for all her heart's endeavour,
    To set its struggling passion free
        From pride, and vainer ties dissever,
25   And give herself to me forever.
    But passion sometimes would prevail,
        Nor could tonight's gay feast restrain
    A sudden thought of one so pale
        For love of her, and all in vain:

30   So, she was come through wind and rain.
Be sure I looked up at her eyes
     Happy and proud; at last I knew
Porphyria worshipped me: surprise
     Made my heart swell, and still it grew
35   While I debated what to do.
That moment she was mine, mine, fair,
     Perfectly pure and good: I found
A thing to do, and all her hair
     In one long yellow string I wound
40   Three times her little throat around,
And strangled her. No pain felt she;
     I am quite sure she felt no pain.
As a shut bud that holds a bee,
     I warily oped her lids: again
45   Laughed the blue eyes without a stain.
And I untightened next the tress
     About her neck; her cheek once more
Blushed bright beneath my burning kiss:
     I propped her head up as before
50   Only, this time my shoulder bore
Her head, which droops upon it still:
     The smiling rosy little head,
So glad it has its utmost will,
     That all it scorned at once is fled,
55   And I, its love, am gained instead!
Porphyria's love: she guessed not how
     Her darling one wish would be heard.
And thus we sit together now,
     And all night long we have not stirred,
60   And yet God has not said a word!

'Porphyria's Lover' by Robert Browning (1836)

>> Task 10.6

Discuss this poem with a partner or in a group to exchange ideas and tease out what it means. Then write a detailed appreciation – an essay commenting on what you find interesting in it – of this poem.

Mention:

- the events in the poem
- the feelings expressed
- the choice of the murderer as narrator
- vocabulary
- rhyme and rhythm
- other poetic devices such as metaphors and what they contribute to the poem.

Writing about literature

Study this example of how you might comment critically on two sentences from *Wuthering Heights*. Brontë's language is very rich. You will probably not be surprised to learn that she was an accomplished poet as well as a novelist.

> Half-a-dozen four-footed fiends of various sizes and ages, issued from hidden dens to the common centre. I felt my heels and coat-laps peculiar subjects of assault; and, parrying off the larger combatants with the poker, I was constrained to demand, aloud, assistance from some of the household, in re-establishing peace.

This passage is a very colourful and poetic way of saying 'I was threatened by several dogs, fended them off with a poker and had to call for help.' Brontë's alliterative 'four footed fiends' creates a real impression of menace and of Lockwood's fear. There is a feeling of the animals pouring out at him from all directions in the word 'issued' too. In the second sentence the words 'peculiar' (used here in the sense of particular rather than odd), 'parrying' and 'poker' are alliteratively linked which evokes the stuttering of Lockwood's panic – and outrage at being made so unwelcome. There is also something faintly comic and pompous about describing the beasts as 'combatants' and using the words 'was constrained' rather than 'had' or 'decided'. Lockwood is evidently taking himself rather more seriously than his host does.

Task 10.7

Choose two sentences from any of the prose extracts in this chapter and write about them in detail.

Personal Writing

>> Task 10.8

1. Write, for teenage readers, a detailed review of any film you have seen recently. Use Passage A as a model.

2. Describe an occasion when you were very ill at ease (as Lockwood is in Passage C).

3. Write a short story or a poem entitled 'Subtle, false and treacherous'.

4. Imagine you are King Leopold telling his parliament about your plans for the Congo. Write the speech. You could consult Hitler's speech in Passage B for ideas about how to be convincing, although yours (Leopold's) can be shorter.

5. Write an essay setting out your views about children working today. They no longer sweep chimneys or (in Britain) work in factories and mines. But many children do paper rounds and other work. Some work part-time as actors in plays, TV shows and so on, for example. And in some developing countries very young children still have to work like adults (making clothing for export for instance) as they did in Britain in the 19th century and before.

6. Write a poem or a story in which the narrator is a villain.

7. You are a (British) news reporter in 1934. You have just received the transcript of Hitler's speech. Write your 400-word front page story for tomorrow's paper.

8. Write about villainy – or subtlety, falsity and treachery – in any way you wish.

Writing tip

When you are writing dialogue try to make it more interesting and less repetitive by using words other than 'said' to explain who is speaking. There are many other possibilities, some of them quite colourful, such as:

whispered	averred	stated
bellowed	opined	requested
demanded	questioned	murmured
muttered	asked	breathed
enquired	exclaimed	declaimed
suggested	proposed	wondered
shouted	mumbled	grumbled
growled	groaned	announced
asserted	observed	intimated

Make dialogue as punchy as you can. Sometimes, if two characters are speaking alternately in short sentences, you don't need explanatory words to tell the reader who is speaking. This has the effect of making the dialogue run very fast down the page and is good, for example, for arguments.

WORD BANK

We have talked a lot about the origins of words – etymology – in this book.

The word **ghoulish** (or its variants) occurs in the passages above more than once. It comes from an Arabic word *ghul* – **a spirit which seized children**.

Words beginning gh- come from various sources. **Ghost** and **ghastly** developed from Old English (see page 112).

Other gh words from elsewhere include: **gherkin** from Dutch, **ghetto** from Italian and **ghee** from Hindi.

Many gn- and kn- words, on the other hand, derive from Old English. These include: **gnome**, **gnat**, **gnaw**, **gnash**, **gnarl**, **knife**, **knee**, **knave**, **knight**, **knock**, **know**.

But gn- words such as **gnostic** come from Ancient Greek and **gnu** comes form Xhosa – an African language. So you cannot generalise with etymology.

➤➤ Task 10.9

Use a good dictionary which gives the etymological history of words. Look up and make notes on what the following words mean and how they came into English:

1. murderer
2. villain
3. tyrant
4. despot
5. blood
6. homicide

>> Task 10.10

All these words come from the passages above. Write one sentence for each to show that you understand its meaning. Then check that you know the spelling of each. Use other forms of the words if you wish.

1. eclectic
2. perverse
3. mutinous
4. judicial
5. precursor

6. neophytes
7. plethora
8. philanthropy
9. vexatious
10. vigilant

11. unremorseful
12. transgression
13. endeavour
14. prevail
15. annihilates

NUTS AND BOLTS Nouns which have come into English via other languages often have specific plurals which have to be learned. For example:

singular	*plural*
crisis	crises
phenomenon	phenomena
stimulus	stimuli
plateau	plateaux
cherub	cherubim
radius	radii
oasis	oases
datum	data
antenna	antennae
appendix	appendices (medical)
	appendixes (of a book)

>> Task 10.11

Write the plural forms of these words. Check in a good dictionary if you need to.

stratum
thesis
seraph
terminus
medium

fungus
automaton
criterion
tempo

Note: some of these 'foreign imports' are gradually being Anglicised. Many dictionaries now, for example, regard **hippopotamuses** as an acceptable alternative plural to **hippopotami** or **formulas** instead of **formulae**. The most important thing to remember is that common words such as **criteria**, **phenomena**, **media**, **graffiti** and **data** are plural. They therefore need plural verb forms. For example:

- Six different criteria govern the judging panel's decisions.

- Personal data are stored (and sometimes lost) by the Government.

- Which media are to be represented at the meeting?

Another group of plurals to be careful of are certain compound nouns (some of which have hyphens) such as brother-in-law, runner-up, and spoonful.

singular	*plural*
manservant	menservants
runner-up	runners-up
teaspoonful	teaspoonsful
chucker-out	chuckers-out
passer-by	passers-by
sister-in-law	sisters-in-law
man-at-arms	men-at-arms

>> Task 10.12

Write the plural forms of these words:

son-in-law	coat-of-arms
tablespoonful	bucketful
maid-of-honour	looker-on
court-martial	mother-in-law

Book titles should be underlined in your writing. Or, if you are typing, use italics. Thus:

I enjoyed reading <u>Dissolution.</u>

<u>Macbeth</u> is our class play this term.

The Rattlebag, an anthology edited by Seamus Heaney and Ted Hughes, includes some remarkable poems.

My mother says that *Jane Eyre* is her favourite book.

This is important, especially when you are writing about literature, because you often have to distinguish between an eponymous hero or heroine and the title of the book or play itself. Correct punctuation makes it clear. It is a matter of accuracy.
For example:

> The finest production of *Othello* I've seen had Chiwetel Ejiofor as Othello although Ewan MacGregor was a disappointing Iago.

> *Emma* was Jane Austen's favourite novel but she didn't expect readers to like Emma.

Do NOT use inverted commas to mark off titles of whole books and other works. Use them only for titles of shorter items within books – such as poems, short stories, chapter headings, essays and so on.
For example:

> Gerard Manley Hopkins's 'Inversnaid' is included in The Rattlebag.

> One of the best short stories in The Jungle Book is 'Riki-Tiki-Tavi'.

> If I had to recommend a single piece from *Essays* by George Orwell it would be 'Politics and the English Language'.

> Every chapter in *Great Expectations* is beautifully written, but 'Walworth Sunday' is perhaps the finest of all.

Whatever you may have been taught when you were younger the rules explained here are the grown-up convention. It is used in all universities and workplaces. So get into good habits now!

More speaking and listening activities

Prepare a dramatic reading of 'Porphyria's Lover' and perform it to a group or the rest of the class. If you can learn it by heart so much the better.

Read one of the books in the 'Wide Range Reading' section of this chapter. Tell the rest of the class about it as an oral review.

Listen to an audiotape of a reading of *Wuthering Heights*. There are several available to buy or borrow through libraries.

The passages in this chapter feature various 'subtle, false and treacherous' people: Sweeney Todd, King Leopold, Hitler, Heathcliff, Grimes and Porphyria's Lover. Discuss in a group which one seems to you to be the worst. One member of the group should then act as the group's spokesperson by summarising the discussion and its conclusions for the rest of the class.

With a partner work out and rehearse a dramatisation of the *Wuthering Heights* extract. One of you should be Lockwood and the other Heathcliff.

An acrostic game

Take a word and make a suitable phrase or sentence from its initial letters.

For example:

- **s**harp **h**and-**o**perated **v**ertical **e**arth **l**ifter (shovel)

- **s**limy **n**octurnal **a**nimal **i**nvading **l**ettuces (snail)

- **b**ox **r**etaining **a**ssorted **i**nteresting **n**otions (brain)

A competition in the magazine *The New Statesman* asked for entries based on the names of plays and films. These were some of the suggestions:

- **J**ust **a** **w**hite **s**hark (Jaws)

- **S**pace, **t**ime **a**nd **r**elativity **w**ith **a** **r**idiculous **s**cript (Star Wars)

- **M**urky **a**trocities **c**ommitted **b**y **e**asily **t**empted **h**usband (Macbeth)

- **T**his **h**as **e**verything: **s**yrupy **o**utbursts, **u**plifting **n**annies, **d**ancing **o**ver **f**lowery **m**ountains, **u**nctuous **s**ongs **i**nvolving **c**hildren (The Sound of Music)

Try this bit of fun with any word or title you like. If you can't think of any starting points try:

- your name or a friend's

- a word such as breakfast, coat, pencil or cabbage

- the name of your school

- a title such as *Bambi*, *Oliver Twist*, *Ratatouille* or *Peter Pan*.

WIDE RANGE READING

The Keys to the Street by Ruth Rendell (1996). This novel is a very readable crime 'thriller' by an author who really knows her business. It tells the story of a con-man trying to get money from a young woman in London. At the same time there is a murderer at large. If you enjoy this there are many more Ruth Rendell novels to move on to. She also writes under the name Barbara Vine.

The Woman in White by Wilkie Collins (1860). Sir Percy Glyde is the subtle, false and treacherous villain in this novel. He marries a young woman for her money and then attempts to dispose of her. The novel has an interesting cast of other characters including Count Fosco. It is told by several different narrators.

Jamaica Inn by Daphne du Maurier (1936). Joss is the eighteenth landlord of a pub on the lonely Bodmin Moor in Cornwall. His niece comes to live with her uncle and aunt and quickly realises that there are sinister things going on at Jamaica Inn for which selling drinks is just a cover. Daphne du Maurier lived in Cornwall and loved it. She is very good at capturing the atmosphere of Cornwall, especially as it would have been in the past.

The Godfather by Mario Puzo (1969). The New York based Corleone family is descended from Sicilian migrants. In Sicily its members were part of the Mafia – the criminal group that controls life through bribes, threats, and murder if necessary. Now very rich, they still control their compatriots in New York. This novel won America's greatest literary award, the Pulitzer Prize, for its author. It is very much better than the (very violent) film which was made from it.

10 Rillington Place by Ludovic Kennedy (1961). This book is not fiction. It is an account of one of the worst ever failures of British justice. John Christie was a serial murderer who lived at 10 Rillington Place in London – the house has long since been demolished. After bodies were discovered in the house his upstairs tenant, Timothy Evans, was hanged for the murders on Christie's evidence. Later the mistake was realised and Christie was tried and also hanged. Ludovic Kennedy is a lawyer and journalist who pieced together all the information to tell the full truth in this fascinating book.

Coram Boy by Jamila Gavin (2002). Written for young adult readers this is a very readable story set in the 18th century about a family in Gloucestershire, the famous Coram Hospital in London and the links between them. Otis is a terrible man. He collects unwanted babies from unmarried mothers, promising to take them to the new orphanage in London. But he doesn't. Then, later in the story, he re-emerges in a different situation still exploiting children in a dreadful way.

A Kind of Wild Justice by Bernard Ashley (1978). Inspired by the real life Kray twins who terrorised many people in London's East End in the 1950s and 60s – rather like the Mafia in Sicily – this novel tells the story of a little boy whose father is at the mercy of the villainous Bradshaw brothers. It is very sensitively and thoughtfully done. Like Coram Boy it was written for young adults.

- • Research the story of Sweeney Todd. Several journalists have written about it and you can easily find their thoughts on the internet. Then decide whether you think it is fact or fiction – or a mixture.

- • Read Ruth Rendell's short story 'Lizzie's Lover'. First published in *Blood Lines* (1995), it is also in *Collected Stories 2* by Ruth Rendell (2008). It is inspired by 'Porphyria's Lover'.

- • Find out about the life of Robert Browning. It is rather colourful and romantic!

- • Read some of Emily Brontë's poetry – perhaps with a partner.

READY FOR A REAL CHALLENGE?

Find out about some or all of these men and what they did: Captain Robert Campbell (Glencoe, 1692), General Reginald Dyer (Amritsar, 1919), General Claus von Stauffenberg (Rastenberg, 1944), King Richard I (Acre, 1191). Do you think they were subtle, false and treacherous? Were they villains? To what extent can their actions and decisions be justified?

Chapter 1 Just for fun

1. Cymbeline, Macbeth
2. Animal Farm
3. Romola, Emma
4. Bleak, Blackbird
5. Macavity, Jennie
6. Tom, Bridget
7. Marner, Uncle
8. Henry, Joyce
9. Hamlet, Kim
10. Harry, Beatrix
11. Anne, Branwell
12. Hawk Roosting

Answer: Jane

Chapter 2 Just for fun

Joseph Conrad	1904	NOSTROMO
Elizabeth Gaskell	1853	RUTH
AS Byatt	1990	POSSESSION
Charlotte Brontë	1859	SHIRLEY
Samuel Butler	1972	EREWHON
Frederick Forsyth	1996	ICON
Benjamin Disraeli	1845	SYBIL
James Joyce	1922	ULYSSES
Ian McEwan	2001	ATONEMENT
Virginia Woolf	1928	ORLANDO

Anagram: NRPSEISUAO **Persuasion** (Jane Austen, 1818)

Chapter 3 Just for fun

This is just a starting point. You will find other words too:

belligerent

beer	bring	grill
bell	enter	grin
bilge	gerbil	leer
bill	girl	line
brine	greet	liner
reel	rent	tern
reeling	retile	tire
reign	rile	trill
rein	ring	tiler
reline	tell	

Chapter 4 Just for fun

1. *Goodnight Mr Tom* by Michelle Magorian
2. *Nicholas Nickleby* by Charles Dickens
3. *Alice in Wonderland* by Lewis Carroll
4. *Harry Potter and the Philosopher's Stone* by JK Rowling
5. *Black Beauty* by Anna Sewell
6. *A Midsummer Night's Dream* by William Shakespeare
7. *The Wind in the Willows* by Kenneth Graeme
8. *The Subtle Knife* by Philip Pullman
9. *Pride and Prejudice* by Jane Austen
10. *Tess of the D'Urberville*s by Thomas Hardy
11. *Kensuke's Kingdom* by Michael Morpurgo
12. *The House at Pooh Corne*r by AA Milne
13. *The Woman in White* by Wilkie Collins
14. *The Silver Sword* by Ian Seraillier
15. *Macbeth* by William Shakespeare
16. *Jane Eyre* by Charlotte Brontë
17. *The Railway Children* by EE Nesbitt
18. *Animal Farm* by George Orwell
19. *The Lion, the Witch and the Wardrobe* by CS Lewis
20. *Skellig* by David Almond

Chapter 5 Just for fun

1. suspension and work
2. racing and boot
3. ash and house
4. red and cleaner
5. capital and suit
6. phone and window
7. fishing and loss
8. spare and arch
9. guide and collar
10. road and post

Answer: glove

Chapter 7 Just for fun

1. *The Family from One End Street*
2. *Two Gentlemen of Verona*
3. *The Three Musketeers*
4. *Crisis Four*
5. *Five Children and It*
6. *Now We Are Six*
7. *The Secret Seven*
8. *Eight Cousins*
9. *To the Nines*
10. *Ten Little Indians* (originally *Ten Little Niggers*)

Chapter 8 Just for fun

1. 'The Highwayman' by Alfred Noyes
2. 'The Lady of Shalott' by Alfred Lord Tennyson (Lord Tennyson or Alfred Tennyson)
3. 'The Pied Piper of Hamelin' by Robert Browning
4. 'The Owl and the Pussy Cat' by Edward Lear
5. 'Sea Fever' by John Masefield
6. 'Daffodils' by William Wordsworth
7. 'Ozymandias' by Percy Byshe Shelley
8. 'The Tyger' by William Blake
9. 'The Listeners' by Walter de la Mare
10. 'Dulce Et Decorum Est' by Wilfred Owen